# A PROBLEM
# SHARED . . .

# A PROBLEM SHARED . . .

A History of the Institute
of London Underwriters
1884 - 1984

by

**CHRIS HEWER**

LONDON
WITHERBY & CO. LTD.
32-36 AYLESBURY STREET
LONDON EC1R 0ET

**Published 1984**
© **Witherby & Co. Ltd. 1984**
✓ **ISBN 0 900886 91 9**  CIRCO

INSURANCE: An ingenious modern game of chance in which the player is permitted to enjoy the comfortable conviction that he is beating the man who keeps the table.

**Ambrose Bierce,**
*The Devil's Dictionary*
(1881-1911)

CHRIS Hewer was born in London in 1948. He worked in the marine cargo departments of a number of leading City brokers before joining *Fairplay International Shipping Weekly* in 1976 as Insurance Correspondent.

He is currently Commercial Editor of *Fairplay*, a regular contributor to leading insurance journals and newsletters, and co-author, with Michael Grey, of *On The Rocks*, an anthology of shipping and insurance humour.

**Publishers note:—**

IT seems appropriate that Witherby & Co. Ltd. should publish and print this history having been suppliers of Institute clauses from their inception and printers to the Institute of London Underwriters since 1884. Will descendants of the present Witherby family be recording events in 100 years from now of similar achievements and progress in the marine insurance industry and by the youthful I.L.U.?

**Alan Witherby,**
Witherby & Co. Ltd. 1740-1984.

# *Acknowledgements*

IN some respects, the preparation of this book has been a simple task. Much of the really hard work had already been done by John Topliss who, before I even sat down at the typewriter, must have spent many long hours rummaging through the Institute's archives in search of relevant information. My debt of gratitude is enormous.

I am greatly indebted also to Fairplay Publications for access to the bound volumes of its *Fairplay International Shipping Weekly* and for permission to publish extracts where appropriate. In addition, part of the preface to this book originally appeared in *Fairplay* under the title "I.L. Who?"

Finally thanks are due to my wife Heather for her invaluable help and encouragement during the preparation of this book, and to Robin and Hannah for making a noise quietly.

**Chris Hewer**

# Contents

# *Foreword*

FOR 39 years I have been married to a barrister — later a judge and Chairman of the Association of Average Adjusters. He has throughout his professional life been closely associated with the marine insurance industry.

So it is with much pleasure that I congratulate the Institute of London Underwriters on 100 years of service to the marine insurance industry and on the publication of this special centenary volume which will doubtless be of great interest to students, enthusiasts and practitioners alike of the art of marine insurance and indeed of shipping in general.

As befits a City with close connections with the sea, London has always been recognised as the centre of international marine insurance, and the expertise of London's marine insurers is acknowledged and valued by other markets throughout the world.

The valuable contribution which the London marine insurance market makes to the invisible earnings of the United Kingdom is continuing evidence of the important part it plays in the economic well-being of the City and of this country.

The commercial interests of the City of London have been served admirably over the years by the representative bodies of their various Institutes. The shipping industry, and those industries which serve it, have been especially well represented in this regard, and none more so than by the I.L.U.

The Institute of London Underwriters can look back on a century of dramatic change and breathtaking developments both in its own sphere and indeed in all walks of life. It has represented the interests of its members in a responsible and progressive manner, and its record speaks for itself. May the next 100 years be equally productive and successful.

**Lord Mayor**
1984

# *Preface*

I HAVE a book which says that St Valentine's Day is a 'festival in celebration of St Valentine, one of the Christian martyrs of the 3rd Century. A sweetheart or Valentine is chosen on that day and letters or tokens sent secretly to the object of affection.'

I wouldn't argue with that, but I wish somebody had told my postman. The only thing he put through the letterbox on February 14th was my Barclaycard statement and a letter for S.W. Short Esq., who moved almost two years ago. *And* he left the gate open. (The postman, that is, not Mr Short).

I have received only one Valentine card in my life and that was hardly sent secretly. I was at primary school, and I can remember the words inside the card as though it were yesterday. "To Chris H" it said, "From Linda S. Do you love *me* best, or Linda G? I must know."

Now the truth of the matter was that, while I thought Linda S a pleasant enough girl, I would have slain dragons for just one smile from the bewitching Linda G. Trouble was, she carried a torch for one Dennis Carpenter, a beastly, gangling youth with green teeth, ears like the F.A. Cup, and breath like a hyena's armpit. What the lovely Linda G saw in him I'll never know, especially as he wasn't in the football team and couldn't play the triangle to save his life, but there you are. I had finally to admit defeat when she wrote his name in biro on her white gym shoes, "Dennis" on the left foot and "Carpenter" on the right. I'm not going to tell you this was the reason I flunked the Eleven Plus, but it didn't help. At any rate, Linda G passed hers and I never saw her again. Linda S moved away and I suspect that she never really forgave me. It may be that she has got over it by now, of course, but her Valentine card lives on. "To Chris H" indeed. The girl had taste.

Let's face it, we all need to be appreciated at times, secretly or otherwise, which is why I felt particularly sorry for certain leading marine underwriters at a recent Annual General Meeting of the Institute of London Underwriters. There were more than a few who were a little peeved at reading that morning in a national newspaper that almost all marine risks are written 100 per cent at Lloyd's, with ILU companies chipping in for a bit of reinsurance if necessary. To those unfamiliar with the structure of the London insurance market, it should be explained that this is roughly equivalent to saying that the Americans won the Second World War.

The truth of the matter is that the ILU, with over 100 member companies, accounts for approximately half of all marine business placed in London. Indeed, most sizeable risks in the London market are placed with a mixture of Lloyd's and Company security and it is the unique capacity and expertise generated by the two markets that has enabled London to remain as the undisputed centre of the marine insurance world.

I doubt that the underwriters at the ILU were looking for any Valentine cards, but they must have been disappointed at being portrayed as the poor relations of the London market. They are not, and it is unfortunate that this misconception should (not for the first time incidentally) have been placed before a large public. Nobody deserves that. Not even Dennis Carpenter.

In 1887, Lord Acton, for reasons best known to himself, wrote that "History provides neither compensation for suffering nor penalties for wrong." It would be expecting too much to right within these pages the wrongs which have been perpetrated over the years. Nor do I think we should try. All we can hope to do is to record the history of one of the world's great commercial institutions in as faithful a way as we know how.

It has always seemed to me that the I.L.U., in sharing its problems among its members, has (if not halved them) then at least reduced them to manageable proportions. If in the process of looking back we can generate some warmth of feeling for the times we speak of, a longing almost for the past, it will not necessarily be a bad thing. The wheel will ever turn a full circle.

**Chris Hewer**

# Chapter 1

# Genesis

IN 1884, Britain was the dominant force in world shipbuilding, launching over three-quarters of the world's tonnage. There were still as many ships operating under sail as there were powered by steam. You could buy a house for £2 a month and you could travel from England to Canada by sea for seven guineas, or five guineas if you were prepared to go steerage. Shipowners in the City were employing clerks at £20.00 per annum, and insurance companies included in their advertisements such promises as "Low Premiums. Large Bonuses. Immediate Payment of Claims." Lloyd's underwriters were grumbling that no money would be made that year. One commentator remarked at the time that "The premiums have been too low. Some companies see this and are writing more carefully, preferring a small premium to a large one with comparatively larger risks."

This was the year, then, in which the Institute of London Underwriters was born, so bringing to a close a curious and frustrating period of monopoly-controlled marine underwriting by British insurance companies. In 1720, the London Assurance Corporation and the Royal Exchange Assurance Corporation had been granted charters and were given a monopoly to insure marine risks in London. But the two companies, despite apparently paying King George I handsomely for the privilege, appeared at this stage to have posed no serious competition to Lloyd's in connection with marine business. A select Commons committee estimated that, at the end of the 18th century, less than four per cent of marine business placed in Britain was insured by either of the two corporations.

There followed in the early years of the nineteenth century several unsuccessful attempts by various bankers and merchants to have the monopoly repealed, but it was not until 1824 that an Act of Parliament, strongly supported by the Prime Minister, Lord Liverpool, brought an end to the monopoly and granted the freedom to establish marine insurance companies. The splendidly named Nathan Meyer Rothschild had, together with some friends, been the prime mover behind the repeal. But, ironically, the company they founded, the Alliance Fire & Life, was prevented from writing marine business by the action of a shareholder. By

# A Problem Shared . . .

the time an independent Alliance Marine Insurance Company had been formed, the Indemnity Mutual Marine Insurance had succeeded in becoming the first new company to write marine insurance following the repeal of the 1720 Act.

There then followed a period of what can only be described as growth-and-collapse. Six new companies were formed between 1824 and 1836, but none lasted more than a few years. In 1845, a boom time for the flotation of limited liability companies, no less than thirteen new marine insurance companies were formed, only one of which survived until 1848. Things then were relatively quiet until 1859, when six new companies were registered, but the only survivor among these was destined to be the Ocean Marine.

The American Civil War was the cause of a boom in marine insurance. A number of very successful companies were formed in the 1860s, and a period of expansion in overseas trade during the latter part of the nineteenth century further boosted the numbers and the strength of the marine insurance companies operating in London. By 1884, some sixty years after the abolition of the monopoly, the company market in London was well established.

Co-operation between the companies at this time was very much on an *ad hoc* basis. In July 1883, a meeting of the "Underwriting Community of the United Kingdom" assembled to hear a report concerning the details and phraseology of certain clauses in general use in marine insurance policies. The committee presenting the report consisted of three Lloyd's underwriters, two representatives each from the Liverpool Underwriters' Association, the Glasgow Underwriters' Association, and the General Shipowners' Society, two merchants and two marine insurance brokers. Three company underwriters (A Tozer of Universal Marine, E.F. Gedge of Royal Exchange Assurance and H.J. Bristow from the Australian & New Zealand Underwriters' Association) made up the committee.

Since the 1850s, senior members of marine insurance companies had been meeting informally in the Jerusalem Coffee House or the Jamaica Wine Rooms near the Royal Exchange to discuss policy wordings and other matters of mutual interest, and it was perhaps inevitable that a representative underwriting association would be formed which would operate under far wider terms of reference than the coffee house committees had ever been able to.

The records show that a proposal to establish an Underwriters' Institute in London was first made in July, 1882, but it was a full year before the chairman of Lloyd's convened a meeting at which it was decided to establish a committee with a mandate to proceed with plans and prepare a Memorandum of Association. The committee met many times in the ensuing weeks but in December 1883 it was found that the proposed memorandum and articles of association were too narrow to enable Lloyd's to continue with negotiations. Colonel Henry M. Hozier, Secretary of Lloyd's at the time, wrote that "It was . . . found necessary that the Institute of London Underwriters, to which Lloyd's wished every success, should be formed on an independent basis. This Institute was accordingly established and took up its abode in the Royal Exchange Buildings." So was born what was to develop into the organisation which today represents the interests of well over 100 marine insurance companies.

No. *19900* C.

N.L. *19247*

# Certificate of Incorporation

OF THE

*Institute of London Underwriters*

# I hereby Certify, That the

*Institute of London Underwriters (the word "Limited" being omitted by Licence of the Board of Trade)*

is this day Incorporated under the Companies' Acts, 1862 to 1883, and that this Company is **Limited**.

Given under my hand at London, this ___*Fifth*___ day of ___*June*___ One Thousand Eight Hundred and Eighty ___*four*___

*Ernest Moore.*

*Assistant* - Registrar of Joint Stock Companies.

Fee: *£5.*

4

# Chapter 2

# The Early Years

THE Institute of London Underwriters received a certificate of incorporation dated June 5, 1884, following the signing of the Articles of Association on May 30 that year. The subscribers to these articles were Henry Joseph Bristow (New Zealand Insurance Co. Ltd.), Edward Davies Brown (Royal Exchange Assurance), Robert John Lodge (Marine Insurance Co. Ltd.), John Henry Lukes (Thames & Mersey Marine Insurance Co. Ltd.), John Stewart Mackintosh (London Assurance), Lawrence Douglas Smith (Indemnity Mutual Marine Assurance Co. Ltd.), and Alfred Tozer (Universal Marine Insurance Co. Ltd.).

The Institute was founded on an independent basis, but observers of the present-day marine insurance market in London may be surprised to know that among the names on the Register of Members for 1884 were Messrs J.W. Janson, Leonard C. Wakefield, Wm. Fred. Saunders, and Marmaduke H. Brooking — Lloyd's underwriters to a man! Furthermore, this was clearly not a freak occurrence confined to the year of incorporation because the records show that Mr. H. Ridgers was elected to membership in 1885 and remained on the Register until 1935.

In those early days, the Institute was not short of characters. None, it seems, was more prolific than Robert Lodge of the Marine Insurance Company. Mr. Lodge, one of the signatories of the ILU's first Articles of Association, brought with him to the Institute a formidable record as an insurance claims investigator. It is a matter of record that the redoubtable Mr. Lodge had on several occasions brought to a successful conclusion complicated and sometimes doubtful claims. His "intelligence, perseverance and tact" in the case of the *Independencia* resulted in a settlement of 35 per cent. Mr Lodge was duly presented with the sum of one thousand guineas by other participating companies as a "slight token of our sense of his invaluable services."

In September, 1857, the slight token had risen to a level of £2,000 following Mr Lodge's investigation into a claim for the loss of a cargo of dollar currency allegedly carried on the *W.J. Sayward*. The letter sent to him on behalf of other subscribers to the risk noted that his enquiries "ultimately defeated a deep-laid plot and baffled the villain who hoped to profit by it." Some of the vessel's crew were traced and confessed that the

*The I.L.U. Certificate of Incorporation dated 5th June, 1884.*

5

ship was scuttled in calm weather off some islands between San Fransisco and China. The boxes supposedly containing dollar coins were allegedly packed with "lead for the weight, and nails for the rattle."

In 1861, Robert Lodge was presented with a cheque for £1,000 for his efforts in exposing an attempt to claim for the loss of gold carried on board the *Matias Cousino*. Mr Lodge sounds as if he would have made a splendid right-hand man for Eric Ellen in today's International Maritime Bureau, and those of us who had fondly imagined that marine underwriters' problems with fraudulent activity began with the *Salem* case will doubtless be obliged to revise our thinking.

The Institute's cash book was opened with a record of the first subscriptions paid by members. Between the 20th and 30th June, 1884, the names of the Indemnity and the Royal Exchange & Marine appeared in the book. They were joined on July 4 by that of the Adelaide National and South Pacific Company of New Zealand, and on July 7 by those of Universal Marine, New Zealand Insurance, Ocean Marine, Home & Colonial Marine Insurance, the Canton Insurance Office, the National Commercial Union, Alliance, London & Provincial, City of London, British & Foreign and Thames & Mersey. The Globe Marine Insurance Company paid its subscription on August 23. The annual subscription was £52.10s., and was to remain so until it was increased at the turn of the century to £60. There were exceptions, however, because the records for 1886 show that Messrs. J.W. Janson, M.H. Brooking and W.F. Saunders were registered as individual members each paying a subscription of five guineas.

The Institute began the tenure of its offices in the Royal Exchange Buildings at a quarterly rent of £100. Among other disbursements in July 1884 were £2.12s.6d for legal charges, £10.4s.6d for advertising, £3.5s.0d for a doorplate, £2.16s.8d for a clock and £8.2s.0d for a carpet!

It is of interest that Coutts & Co. were appointed the Institute's Banker's from the outset.

The Institute Secretary, C.W. Emson, drew his first salary cheque on July 28, 1884. This was for the princely sum of £25.00. But before the end of the century two assistants had been engaged, each at a starting salary of £2.10s.0d per month. By 1900, the cost to the Institute of staff salaries amounted to £690 per annum. Today, the annual expenditure for salaries and related costs is in excess of £1 million.

The records certainly contain numerous other examples of what might be described as the "careful administration" of the Institute. The first payment to Messrs. Witherby & Co., printers of the Institute clauses and providers of other stationery, was in November 1884 for the sum of £4.11s.0d. The Institute committee did not encourage extravagence, but this was no bad thing since individual insurance companies frequently incurred criticism in the shipping Press of the day if their operating expenses appeared to be excessive.

In the 1880s, the Ocean Marine Insurance Company appeared to be a favourite target of the Press. *Fairplay* had this to say of the Ocean's balance sheet for the year ended December 31, 1884:— "The most objectionable feature about this company to our minds is the enormous expense at which it is conducted. For a premium income of £109,000, earned on a total amount written of £12,371,000, the expenses amount to over £14,000 — that is to say 14 per cent of the premium income. We fail to see how any company in the world, especially one suffering, like the Ocean, from semi-paralysis, can possibly succeed against such charges as these. £4,313 in directors' fees! The amount is absurd, and if the shareholders are alive to their own interests they will take steps to reduce it . . ."

The first Ordinary General Meeting of the Institute took place on November 6, 1884. Mr Lawrence Smith of the Indemnity was in the chair, with the Secretary, Mr Charles W. Emson, signing the report from "4 Royal Exchange Building, London E.C." This report noted that, in its first three months of operation, the Institute had paid particular attention to country damage to cotton, the stowage of coal cargoes and the discharge of nitrate at Dunkirk, while claims for "cargo or stores burnt as fuel . . ." was also discussed and earmarked as the likely subject of a future report. If those underwriters who prepared this report could be allowed a look at the marine insurance market today, they would doubtless be staggered to learn just how little has really changed in the intervening 100 years. These meetings and reports became a regular feature of the Institute's activities, continuing on a monthly frequency until well into 1892.

*The very first Committee Report of the I.L.U. dated 6th October, 1884.*

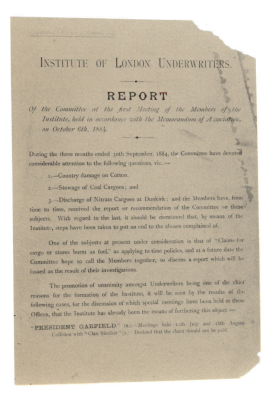

INSTITUTE OF LONDON UNDERWRITERS.

### REPORT

*Of the Committee at the first Meeting of the Members of the Institute, held in accordance with the Memorandum of Association, on October 6th, 1884.*

During the three months ended 30th September, 1884, the Committee have devoted considerable attention to the following questions, viz.:—

1.—Country damage on Cotton.

2.—Stowage of Coal Cargoes; and

3.—Discharge of Nitrate Cargoes at Dunkirk; and the Members have, from time to time, received the report or recommendation of the Committee on these subjects. With regard to the last, it should be mentioned that, by means of the Institute, steps have been taken to put an end to the abuses complained of.

One of the subjects at present under consideration is that of "Claims for cargo or stores burnt as fuel," as applying to time policies, and at a future date the Committee hope to call the Members together, to discuss a report which will be issued as the result of their investigations.

The promotion of unanimity amongst Underwriters being one of the chief reasons for the formation of the Institute, it will be seen by the results of the following cases, for the discussion of which special meetings have been held at these Offices, that the Institute has already been the means of furthering this object:—

"PRESIDENT GARFIELD" (s.)—Meetings held 11th July and 18th August. Collision with "Clan Sinclair" (s). Decided that the claim should not be paid.

"SOLENT" (s.)—Meeting held 22nd July. Collision with "Saintange." Decided to refer the owner to his solicitors, to obtain evidence from both sides.

"TEMPO" (s.)—Meeting held 24th July. Burning of stores for fuel. Settlement declined and claim withdrawn.

"EGYPTIAN MONARCH" (s.)—Meeting held 26th July. Jettison of deck cargo charged in G/A. Decided to object to the adjustment, and to obtain, if possible, concerted action from Liverpool and elsewhere.

"AUSTRAL" (s.)—Meeting held 1st August. Sunk in Sydney Harbour, November, 1882. Decided that no further settlement be made on account until the adjustment is complete.

"CASTLEFORD" (s.)—Meeting held 25th August. Collision with "Rosedale" (s). Decision of Admiralty Court discussed.

"SALERNO" (s.)—Meetings held 8th and 15th September. Jettison of deck cargo charged in G/A. Decided that Messrs. Manley Hopkins & Sons should be requested to amend their statement.

"ADELINE SCHULL" (s.)—Meeting held 25th September. Stranding at Aviles, &c. Information received from the Board of Trade was considered, and the meeting adjourned pending presentation of the average statement.

In addition to the above, a meeting of all the Members was called to consider the following question:—

"Is the whole loss by jettison claimable directly on an f.p.a. policy, or is the claim limited to a contribution to that loss in G/A?"

It was decided to communicate with Lloyds and Liverpool on the question, and representatives have since been appointed from these bodies to meet representatives from this Institute, with a view of deciding upon the principle which should be commended for the adoption of Underwriters generally in dealing with such cases.

CHARLES W. EMSON,
*Secretary.*

4, ROYAL EXCHANGE BUILDINGS,
LONDON, E.C.

# A Problem Shared . . .

From the earliest days, the Institute took a dominant role in trying to improve a variety of clauses in general use. For example, an amended Running Down Clause, a Seaworthy Clause and a Coal Clause were introduced in December 1884, and members agreed that the revised Running Down Clause would be attached to all hull policies after January 1, 1885.

In the report for May 1885, the responsibility of underwriters for damage to machinery arising from the negligence of engineers was declared to be a matter of urgent importance. The increase in claims of this nature had made it necessary to obtain a final decision on this issue, and underwriters in Liverpool had resolved to bring before the courts as a test case the dispute involving the steamer *Inchmaree*, which was destined to become one of the most significant vessels in the history of marine insurance.

In 1884, the *Inchmaree* was filling her boilers off Diamond Island, Burma, when, as a result of the failure of the engineers to establish whether an inlet check valve was open or not, water which was consequently unable to enter the boiler split the air-chamber of the ship's pump which was being worked by a donkey engine. Some minor damage was caused to an air-chamber, and although the trial court and the Court of Appeal decided that the damage was covered by the ordinary wording of the policy, the House of Lords ultimately ruled that underwriters should be relieved of liability.

At a general meeting of the I.L.U. in April 1885, it had been unanimously decided that the Thames and Mersey Marine Insurance Company should be authorised to act on behalf of the underwriting community, and a committee of supervision was appointed to manage the case. It is possible that the dispute may never have reached the House of Lords, since the committee only agreed to continue the fight when it became clear that the Court of Appeal ruling was not a unanimous one.

The decision in this case (*Hamilton Fraser & Co. v Thames & Mersey*) led to the introduction of the Inchmaree Clause. Although the market had fought for this decision, it was not underwriters' intention that the assured should be without protection against accidents involving machinery, whether caused fortuitously or as a result of negligence. It was not long before the following clause appeared in the market:— 'This insurance also specially to cover loss of or damage to hull and machinery through the negligence of master, mariners, engineers or pilots, or through explosions, bursting of boilers, breakage of shafts, or through any latent defect in the machinery or hull, provided such loss or damage has not resulted from want of due diligence by the owners of the ship, or any of them, or by the manager." Since it was first issued, this Negligence Clause has been amended on a number of occasions to meet varying requirements.

At the monthly meeting of the Institute in March 1886, the Standing Committee appointed by the I.L.U. and Lloyd's to monitor on underwriters' behalf the proceedings of the Royal Commission on Loss of Life at Sea outlined the following resolutions which it felt would assist in the preservation of life and property:—

(1) In cases of Constructive Total Loss, the value upon which the vessel was to be condemned should be the value in the policy.

(2) That there should be an implied warranty of seaworthiness in time policies as well as in voyage policies.

(3) That the value of freight should always be an open one, with net freight only recoverable.

(4) That it was desirable that insurance cases should be tried without a jury.

(5) That deviation to save property as well as life should not vitiate an insurance.

(6) That the power of an owner to insure should not be restricted to less than the indemnity value of his vessel and that no underwriter should be able to open a value sustainable at the commencement of the policy.

(7) That in the event of any claim for loss, underwriters were to have the power to demand particulars of every insurance, legal or otherwise, on the ship, freight, expenses or any other interest of the owner in force at the time of the loss.

(8) That some liability for negligence should remain with the shipowner but that the extent thereof should be limited and that the shipowner should neither be able to contract out of this liability nor cover it by insurance.

These resolutions were subsequently submitted to and unanimously approved by a special meeting of I.L.U. members.

It can readily be seen that, from the very start, the Institute was no mere cosmetic organisation brought together to satisfy undernourished egos in the City. It was in the very vanguard of all the major shipping and marine insurance issues of the day, looking out for the interests of its membership and, together with Lloyd's, representing most ably the insurance industry's viewpoints. It's resolve to be recognised as an effective and responsible representative of its members' interests in the eyes of such strategic bodies as the Royal Commission on Loss of Life and Property at Sea can be gauged by its reaction to the practice which became prevalent in the London market in the 1880s whereby certain non-Institute companies included in their policies cover for liabilities more properly and traditionally borne by the shipowners themselves or their Protection & Indemnity Clubs.

The Institute report for July 1886 contained a resolution which referred to ". . . the draft policy issued by certain insurance companies in

## A Problem Shared . . .

Liverpool, enlarging the conditions of the marine policy so as to include most of the liabilities hitherto borne by the shipowner . . ." Emphasising that this practice was in direct opposition to the principles advocated by the Institute before the Royal Commission, the report said the adoption of such a policy form was not only unnecessary and undesirable but would be "prejudicial to the real interest of all parties concerned."

Another matter which demanded the Institute's attention during 1886 was the unsatisfactory nature of many claims for laying-up returns and the acceptance, in the absence of market support for a more stringent requirement, of the Liverpool clause which provided that ". . . In case of damage that may involve a claim under this policy, notice where practicable to be given to the underwriters in order that they may appoint a representative on their behalf." Work was also undertaken in connection with an interpretation of the phrase "laid up in port" as meaning from the time the vessel was moored for discharge to when she was unmoored after loading but with leave to go into drydock if necessary. Today's underwriters may indeed derive a certain amount of perverse satisfaction from the realisation that they are not alone in having had their problems with laid-up tonnage.

On a constitutional note, 1886 ought not to be allowed to pass without some reference here to the fact that in that year a representative of the National Board of Marine Underwriters, New York, was elected to the Institute and that the Committee took steps to appoint a representative, Mr. A.J. Macdonald of the Thames and Mersey Marine Insurance Company, to act in a similar capacity on their behalf in the United States. This followed an alteration in the Articles of Association enabling foreign and colonial companies to join the Institute at a reduced rate of subscription, but the expected increase in membership from this source did not materialise.

These were years of new and developing trade patterns. A case in point is the frozen meat trade which grew rapidly in the latter part of the 19th century. In 1890 under 3 million carcasses of mutton and lamb were received into the United Kingdom, while nearly 6 million were brought in during 1896. The meat came from a variety of origins, from Australia, New Zealand, the River Plate and the United States. Today's housewife would doubtless blanch a little on learning that Smithfield Market prices in 1884 varied from 4½d to 6½d per lb for New Zealand lamb, and from 3½d to 5¼d for that from Australian origins.

But the growth in the frozen meat trade also brought a spate of heavy claims which prompted an Institute sub-committee to attempt to formulate insurance conditions which would eventually be acceptable to the Frozen Meat Trade Association and yet be of a character which could be recommended to underwriters for general adoption. The meat traders and the underwriters agreed that the Conference Clauses of 1895 should be amended and certain restrictions introduced. Almost all the London and Liverpool companies signed an agreement to adopt the amended clauses, copies of which were forwarded to the colonies for attachment to appropriate policies.

June 1887 brought a change of premises for the Institute. The I.L.U. abandoned its offices in Royal Exchange Buildings, having with its customary frugality first obtained the sum of £7.00 from the new occupants, the Union Fire Assurance Company, in respect of fixtures and fittings left behind. The Institute took up new offices at 1, St. Michael's House, Cornhill, at the lower rent of £68.15s.0d. per quarter, which sum was in fact reduced in 1894 to a quarterly amount of £62.10s.0d.

It was in 1887 also that the I.L.U. committee petitioned for a reduction in the *ad valorem* duty on marine policies to the sum of one penny, irrespective of the amount insured. The Institute companies were joined in this action by their underwriting colleagues in Liverpool and by about twenty of the leading firms of bankers and merchants. But a petition to the Lords of the Treasury met with an unsympathetic response and the duty was destined to remain payable for many years to come.

Two problems which company underwriters were particularly anxious to solve during the early years of the I.L.U.'s existence were the granting of fifteen-day returns and the insertion of valuation clauses in hull policies. Although all the London companies, together with many Lloyd's underwriters, signed an undertaking not to admit returns in policies for time under a limit of 30 days, the Liverpool companies would not agree and the I.L.U. committee members were left to reflect that the practice of allowing fifteen-day returns might never be abolished. They were not to know that an agreement signed in 1915 was largely to achieve this end.

The Institute report for May 1888 drew attention to the advantage to be derived by underwriters from the insertion in hull policies of a clause to the effect that "The insured value to be mutually admitted and taken as the sound value of the ship for all purposes of loss under this policy."

A form of agreement requiring this clause to be inserted in all hull policies was signed by all I.L.U. members, but the Liverpool underwriters again proved to be the stumbling block, refusing to sign an agreement for the general adoption of the clause for fear that it would lead to a reduction in the insured value of vessels and an increase in honour policies against T.L.O. for disbursements etc. So strong was the Liverpool underwriters' objection to a binding agreement of this nature that the I.L.U. committee was forced to acknowledge that no such agreement was at that time possible.

In these formative years of the I.L.U., and indeed throughout the nineteenth century, all manner of inventive, one-off clauses were being drawn up by Lloyd's and company underwriters, by brokers, shipowners, merchants and others, which resulted in some instances in the creation of very diverse versions of the cover which had originally been intended. A collection of all the supplementary clauses in use at the time, drawn up by Sir Douglas Owen and published in 1882 under the title *Marine Insurance Notes and Clauses,* revealed for example that no less than twelve versions existed of the Running Down Clause. It was perhaps not surprising, then, that Sir Douglas was sceptical about the I.L.U.'s efforts to achieve greater uniformity in marine insurance clauses.

Many years were to elapse before the so-called "clauses of the marketplace" were driven out of use, but a major step in the right direction was achieved when the Time Clauses on Hulls were introduced by a London company and issued by the I.L.U. in 1888. These conditions were described as being "recommended by the Institute of London Underwriters for adoption in the year's policies on hulls." (See Appendices)

*The original 1888 and 1889 Time Clauses as recorded by the I.L.U.*

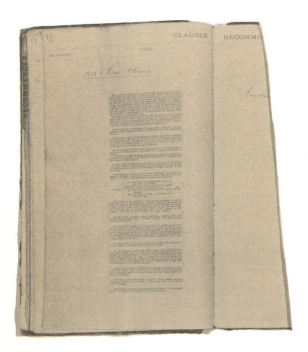

Although the clauses (which strangely enough appear not to have been approved by the committee of the Institute) were found by a special I.L.U. sub-committee to work "on the whole satisfactorily", certain alterations were proposed at the end of 1888. As a result, the "1889 Time Clauses" were followed quickly by the "1890 Clauses." For a few years thereafter, these clauses were issued annually, but in time they were only reissued following the incorporation of specific amendments.

The adoption of the 1889 Time Clauses very quickly resulted in problems of interpretation with regard to that part of the Negligence Clause referring to latent defects. The Institute asked five questions of its solicitors:—

(1) What is a latent defect?

(2) Are underwriters liable for repairing the defect itself, or only the consequences?

(3) Is the owners' superintendent a "manager" under the clause in the case under consideration?

(4) What is the effect of omitting the paragraph "provided such loss or damage has not resulted from want of due diligence by the owners of the ship, or any of them or by the manager"?

(5) Is liability consequent upon discovery?

The opinion of the lawyers was that a latent defect was one which by its nature was not discoverable by any of the ordinary modes of examination. In their opinion, underwriters did not provide the assured with a warranty against the existence of a latent defect at the time the policy attached, nor agree to make good any latent defect then existing. They simply warranted that if the vessel was lost during the period of insurance by reason of a latent defect even previously existing, they would pay for the loss — and if during the period of insurance the vessel sustained further damage as a consequence of any such latent defect, they would pay for this also.

It is strange how some underwriting problems seem to be with us for ever. You will find insurers, lawyers, average adjusters and the like still debating the definition of latent defect today. And a look at the records shows the existence of other persistent problems, because at about this time the Institute committee was expressing concern over the practice of clean bills of lading being issued for goods damaged prior to shipment, upon receipt from the shipper of a letter of indemnity couched in suitably contrived language. How little changes!

There was no shortage of explosions on board vessels at this time, either. One such incident, an explosion in December 1889 on board the 973-ton *Fergusons* which was unloading a petroleum cargo at Rouen, led to a change in the requirements called for by classification societies. An inquiry revealed that the *Fergusons* explosion was caused by a poorly insulated electric light. This was not the first case of the use of electricity

## A Problem Shared . . .

resulting in a fire on board ship, and the Chairman of the I.L.U. was subsequently asked to raise with the committee of Lloyd's Register (of which he was a member) the proposal that the Register Book should contain a notation if the vessel was lighted by electricity and that the installation should be brought under the Rules of Survey. But Bureau Veritas on this occasion acted more quickly than did Lloyd's Register, agreeing to place a distinctive mark against ships fitted with electricity and to prepare a code of rules for the supervision of such fittings. Lloyd's Register complied in part with the request a little while later, but neither society could impose a general code of rules for some time.

In 1890, the Institute took part in two developments of great importance in the shipping world. It was represented at the conference for the revision of the York-Antwerp Rules of 1877, which remained in force from 1890 to 1924, and together with the Committee of Lloyd's and Liverpool underwriters made representations to the Board of Trade in connection with the Merchant Shipping Act of 1890 which provided for the fixing and making of load lines on all British ships. The I.L.U. committee was concerned that competition among classification societies might prejudice the advantages of the Act and duly urged the Board of Trade to delegate its authority in this matter to the committee of Lloyd's Register alone or at least that underwriters should be strongly represented on any other organisation appointed for that purpose.

The records for this period also reveal another problem which will be familiar to today's underwriter — "claims of a very heavy character made against insurance on tank steamers." The Institute pointed out that the building of steamers for the purpose of carrying oil in bulk had been very much in the nature of an experiment and that the experience gained with regard to control and equipment had been a very costly one for insurers. The words have a familiar ring.

*The 1886 built bulker "Gluckhauf", generally regarded as the fore-runner of the modern tanker. Underwriting records in the late 19th century reveal "claims of a very heavy character . . . on tank steamers."*

1891 brought further developments in connection with standard marine conditions, with the addition of the Steamer Voyage Clauses. In 1893, the now familiar headings of Institute Time Clauses and Institute Voyage Clauses were introduced. London Conference Frozen Meat Clauses were first issued in 1895 and the Institute Clauses for Builders Risk appeared in 1899.

Despite these developments, however, a large number of "unofficial" clauses were still circulating in the market. Owners' clauses were in regular use for the insurance of liner fleets and the Institute Builders Risk Clauses were in competition with wordings drafted by shipbuilders and their brokers. But there were some encouraging signs too. Evidence was given before the courts in April 1891 that at least 80 per cent of insurances effected during 1888 were taken out on the 1888 Time Clauses form. There was still a lack of uniformity in the general use of clauses, however, and the Institute, together with the Committee of Lloyd's and the Liverpool Underwriters' Association, prepared a list of clauses to be known as the "London and Liverpool Clauses" which were based on wordings in current use or, if amended in any way, approved by one or more firms of solicitors specialising in shipping and mercantile law.

*The early days of the Institute were marked by dramatic developments in shipping. The 1897 built "Turbinia" was the first vessel in the world to be powered by a steam turbine.*

Mention should be made here of the subject of war and strikes risks. During the 1880s and for most of the next decade, cover had been provided against war risks without charge. But following the outbreak of the Spanish American War in 1898, notice was given that all risks accepted after May 19, 1898, should contain the Free of Capture and Seizure Clause. In October that year, owing to the strained political relations between France and England, all the companies and many Lloyd's underwriters gave notice under their open policies to include the FC&S Clause. Since that time, of course, the Institute has been actively involved in creating and enforcing a wide variety of war risk agreements.

## A Problem Shared . . .

It would be wrong to close this chapter on the nineteenth century without some mention of the levels of rating pertaining in the market. A broker writing to the Editor of *Fairplay* in 1899 said that if a member of the broking fraternity ". . . knew that underwriters were unanimous and solid in their rates, he would send quotations to his clients with every confidence that rival brokers would have no chance of cutting him out. But when I quote 7s.6d. per cent, and another broker solicits an order at 6s.8d. per cent, and succeeds in placing it, where am I?"

The Editor replied that Lloyd's and the companies "should make a stand for 'living' premiums. If the weaker ones, and foreign agencies, run after 10s.6d. business at 7s.6d., let them gorge themselves with it and suffer the penalty . . ." Advice of this sort was destined to be repeated many times in the years ahead.

*Members of the Institute at the Annual General Meeting in 1898.*

16

So at the dawn of the 20th century the Institute could look back on its early years with a considerable sense of achievement. A variety of matters prejudicial to insurers had been brought to the attention of underwriters and steps had been taken by general agreement or otherwise to deal with the problems. Not all the difficulties had been solved quickly or even *solved*, but the important first moves had been made. Had there been no contact and co-operation between the insurance companies of London, there is little doubt that the remedies would have been longer in the making. There could be no more compelling factor which might justify the Institute's existence.

ÆQUITAS ACTIONUM REGULA

18

# Chapter 3

# The New Century

BY the close of the nineteenth century, Queen Victoria was nearing the end of the longest reign in the history of the English monarchy. Her people had known the extremes of poverty and great wealth, of war and peace. Indeed, in 1900, British ships were busily engaged carrying troops to South Africa following the invasion of Natal a few months previously by the Boers. In the months prior to the outbreak of hostilities, marine underwriters in London had been writing slips on total losses in the event of war breaking out at rates in the region of 60 guineas. Queen Victoria was not to see the end of the Boer War, and her death in 1902 brought to an end one of the truly great eras in British history.

At home, against the background of a powerful Empire and an expanding economy, shipbuilding in the United Kingdom was going through a boom period. The Lloyd's Register Returns released in 1900 revealed that the merchant shipbuilding output from UK yards in 1899 had surpassed all earlier records. More significantly, perhaps, the 1899 newbuildings were almost exclusively steamships, whereas only six years previously almost 20 per cent of domestic output was accounted for by sailing vessels. Dramatic changes in the design and the size of ships were destined to create a whole range of problems for underwriters in the years ahead.

In the City, the year 1900 opened to the sound of underwriters at Lloyd's and in the company market maintaining that they were well justified in their stiffening of hull rates and conditions the previous year. The cost of repairs, they said, had become excessive, with wages and materials having reached an abnormally high level. They also argued that the substitution of steel for iron in certain shipbuilding techniques had rebounded unfavourably on their underwriting results, steel-built vessels faring much worse in strandings and heavy collisions than their iron counterparts. One commentator remarked at the time that it was the damage claims, rather than the total loss ones, which were upsetting and scaring underwriters and ruining their calculations. More than eighty years later, the market commentators are still relaying the same message.

Underwriters at this time were being accused of unfairness in their rating approach to cargo carriers, against whom it was alleged they discriminated in favour of the liner operators. Shipping people argued that, if insurers were intent on maintaining this unbalanced approach towards their underwriting, the cargo carriers would be well advised to take their business out of the company offices and the Room and put it into the books of the mutual clubs.

The Liverpool Underwriters' casualty figures released in January, 1900, have a familiarly depressing ring. For the twelve months ending December 31, 1899, the figures recorded a total of 1,020 vessels which had been weather-damaged; 80 founderings and abandonments; 1,295 strandings (including 132 total losses); 1,488 collisions (including 30 total losses); 233 fires and explosions (six total losses); 37 missing; and 1,228 other casualties, giving a total for the year of 5,381 casualties, of which 285 were total losses.

The report of the Institute for 1899, released in January 1900, expressed the opinion that underwriters had been writing the hulls of liners at inadequate rates of premium. The I.L.U. Committee said that it hoped to see a marked improvement in the rates and conditions for the insurance of steamers of the regular lines and for so-called 'semi-liners'. No reference was made to the results of 'tramp' business, thereby providing implied support for those in the shipping industry who argued that inadequate liner premiums were being made good by underwriters' overcharging of the tramps.

In the same report, the Institute called for the valuation clause to be inserted in all hull policies, and urged that when vessels were insured on the understanding that they were employed in certain trades, a warranty be inserted in the policy preventing them from going into more dangerous trades without the payment of an additional premium. The valuation clause was a classic example of a prudent underwriting approach which inevitably attracted criticism from within the shipping industry. This has become an occupational hazard for marine insurers over the years.

It was said that the valuation clause was very one-sided, stating as it did that the estimated cost of repairs had to amount to or exceed the policy value, or the vessel could not be condemned. In the absence of the clause, a vessel was considered to be a constructive total loss when the estimated amount of repairs exceeded the ship's value when repaired. Shipping interests felt that the valuation clause placed an unfair burden on the shipowner, and it was argued that underwriters should reduce the test of constructive total loss under the clause from 100 per cent of the insured value to perhaps 80 per cent or thereabouts.

Certainly the situation in 1900 appears not to have been so different from that which pertains today. An alarming casualty toll, insufficient premium to satisfy those discerning underwriters who could see beyond moderate years of business to the need to build up reserves, and the eternal

*the late 19th cen-*
*·y, there were still as*
*ıny ships operating*
*der sail as there were*
*·wered by steam. The*
*J2-built "Preussen"*
*s the only five-*
*ısted full-rigged ship*
*·r built.*

difficulty of finding solutions acceptable to both the shipping and the insurance industry. For those who might be looking for a clue to the premium rates of the day, it was rumoured that the American liner *Paris* had been insured for £120,000 from Milford Haven to Belfast, while undergoing repairs there, and back to Southampton, the larger part of the value at 30s. and the remainder at 40s. per cent.

# A Problem Shared . . .

*The liner "Paris"*
*aground off Cornwall*
*in 1901 — the larger*
*part insured at 30s. per*
*cent.*

## A Problem Shared . . .

The annual meeting of the company and Lloyd's underwriters to consider the Institute Time & Voyage Clauses for 1903 met at the end of 1902, and reaffirmed the clauses without alteration. This followed several years of alteration to the standard conditions, including one reissue of the clauses without the Continuation Clause following the well publicised *Merrimac* case and then a further reissue with a new Continuation Clause after the Government had introduced provision in its Finance Bill to legalise the use of the clause upon the payment of additional stamp duty of sixpence. This development came about as a result of representations made by underwriters and a shipowners' association.

At the corresponding meeting of underwriters in 1904, a committee was appointed to prepare "Institute Time Clauses, Hulls F.P.A. absolutely". A committee was also appointed to consider the question of Institute Warranties, and amendments were made extending the liberties of the assured.

Another problem discussed at the conference was the now familiar one of the great loss of premium arising from the practice of allowing returns for fifteen days instead of the thirty days provided by the Institute Clauses. A resolution was passed deprecating the practice, and this met with such general approval that its adoption in both London and Liverpool was thought to be assured. In the same year, Institute Time Clauses for Freight were introduced in order to clear up any misunderstanding which had previously arisen in connection with freight insurances.

In 1906, "An Act to Codify the Law relating to Marine Insurance", known more commonly as the Marine Insurance Act, was placed on the Statute Book. The drafting of the Bill had in the main been the work of Judge Chalmers, whose proposals had over a number of years been submitted to a committee of shipowners, lawyers, average adjusters and underwriters, on which the Institute was ably represented. The Act basically codified previous legal decisions and customary practices relating to marine insurance. It also approved the use of the S.G. Policy Form which, despite being the subject of so much criticism and abuse over the years, was to survive in its original format until almost the present day.

In the same year, British underwriters came to a decision which was to lead to difficulties and embarrassment some years later. At about this time, observers of the international situation became anxious at the various sabre-rattling activities of the German Emperor and other prominent Germans and at the marked build-up of German naval forces. Underwriters became concerned about the effect that certain newspaper articles might have upon those of their assureds who were non-British nationals, and particularly those who were subjects of the German Empire. In an effort to minimise the suggestion of any possible risk of non-payment of outstanding liabilities to these assureds in the event of hostilities breaking

*A sign of changing times for shipping and for underwriters — the 1905-built "Archibald Russell" was the last sailing ship to trade under British owner-ship.*

out between Great Britain and Germany, British underwriters declared that they would fulfill their obligations, in times of peace as well as war, under contracts they had concluded in the German Empire. Future events were to show how much better it would have been if this declaration, however sincerely and honourably made, had never been issued.

In 1908, the Institute Committee gave a great deal of attention to the growing problem of those people who had no interest in a particular risk but who took out Policy Proof of Interest (P.P.I.) policies. A meeting was held at the Board of Trade on December 15, presided over by the Rt. Hon. Winston Spencer Churchill. The Institute was represented by its chairman, Mr R.B. Lemon, who expressed the disapproval of under-writers of the actions of those individuals who, despite having no genuine interest in marine risks, were effectively gambling by taking out insurance on merchant ships, to the detriment of shipowners and others and at the possible risk of the lives of officers and crew.

At the meeting, attended by four representative underwriters and four representative shipowners, there was a broad consensus of opinion that the gamblers, or "spotters" as they were called, should no longer be afforded the protection of P.P.I. policies to encourage their speculative activities, but that those people with a legitimate interest in the risk should not be deprived of the protection of the policy.

The Board of Trade meeting was adjourned without any firm resolution being passed. Indeed, it was reported that, whilst some underwriters felt that the activities of the gamblers were definitely on the increase, others were of the opinion that the extent of gambling by outsiders had been

# A Problem Shared . . .

greatly exaggerated. But there was no doubt that the underwriting community was firmly against the spotters, and the I.L.U. Committee asked all underwriters to unite in putting a stop to the practice. In the following year, the Marine Insurance (Gambling Policies) Act 1909 was passed, so putting an end to these serious abuses without interfering with legitimate insurance practices.

*Still a demand for sail — the 1909-built "Wyoming" was the largest wooden vessel ever built.*

It seems that underwriters in the early part of the 20th century were as concerned about fraudulent claims as are their present-day counterparts. A typical example from the period involved the Turkish vessel *Mabrouk,* in connection with which an insurance was effected on specie for the sum of £400,000. The vessel was to carry gold in barrels from Beirut to Marseilles. Underwriters were told that the cargo was to be declared to the Customs authorities as "old iron" because the export of gold was prohibited. The vessel was reported sunk shortly after sailing. The underwriters decided to send a special representative, Joseph Lowrey, to make enquiries into the circumstances of the loss. Mr Lowrey, claims adjuster with the Merchants Marine Insurance Company, found that the *Mabrouk* was an open boat loaded with a few barrels and then taken out to sea and scuttled. The wreck was located and the barrels found to contain iron. The assured was notified through the brokers who placed the risk that if he wished to collect his claim he must do so in person. The record does not show if the assured took up this invitation!

In the first decade of the 20th century, the Institute played its full part in drafting and issuing sets of clauses. By 1908, the following Institute Clauses and Warranties were in use:—

Institute Clauses — Hulls F.P.A. absolutely
Institute Clauses — Hulls — Free of Damage absolutely
Institute Clauses — Builders' Risks
Institute Lake Time Clauses — Hulls
Institute Lake Time Clauses — Protection & Indemnity Clause
Institute Warranties — Hulls

The first set of clauses designed for a particular type of cargo to be adopted, meanwhile, were the "London Conference Frozen Meat Clauses, July 1895." Other clauses for the insurance of specific types of cargo had over the years been introduced by various underwriters. But it was thought that standard cargo clauses should be drafted to replace the numerous wordings used by brokers and, as a preliminary to such standardisation, a number of firms of brokers were asked in 1908 to provide copies of clauses used for the insurance of cargo.

Sets of cargo clauses drawn up respectively by S. Kennard Davis and C.F. Jarvis were circulated for the consideration of the I.L.U. Committee in March, 1909. These clauses were forwarded to the Liverpool Underwriters' Association and the Manchester Marine Insurance Association. The secretary of the latter organisation replied that "... I was instructed to thank you ... and to state that the said clauses as a whole were considered to be scarcely suitable for the Manchester market." And although Liverpool considered that "the selection made meets the object in view", Lloyd's underwriters were unable to agree with the clauses in question and the matter was apparently shelved. But within four years the 'Institute Cargo Clauses' were to be passed by the market.

The I.L.U. Committee was proving its worth more impressively with each passing year, and a typical example of its prompt action occurred early in 1911 following a number of serious fires which broke out in Custom House buildings and warehouses at Buenos Aires and Montevideo which resulted in heavy losses for underwriters. An agreement was reached by London and Liverpool companies as well as by a large number of Lloyd's underwriters not to accept any new business to the River Plate or to renew existing contracts unless subject to the proviso that the insurance would cease upon arrival at any shed, store, Custom house or warehouse or upon the expiry of 10 days subsequent to landing, whichever might first occur. This was known as the River Plate Agreement.

The first decade of the 20th century saw severe competition in marine insurance markets, with rates constantly being reduced. But the I.L.U. Committee was able to report that, towards the close of 1908, rates for

## A Problem Shared . . .

both hulls and cargoes had hardened considerably and that there was a greater tendency on the part of underwriters to act together for their mutual benefit. Nevertheless, a later eminent underwriter and I.L.U. Chairman, on leaving school during this period, apparently sought and was offered employment with a marine insurance company, but was warned by the company secretary that conditions were such in the market that no guarantee of a future career in marine insurance could be promised!

*The 'unsinkable' "Titanic" — insured for £1m but thought to be valued nearer £1.5m.*

In the latter part of 1911 and the early part of 1912, those words might have been viewed as an understatement, since this period was blighted by a monstrous succession of disasters involving underwriters in heavy losses, the most famous of which involved the "unsinkable" liner *Titanic*. The *Titanic* was insured for hull and machinery risks to the tune of £1m, but the value of the vessel was thought to be nearer £1.5m, so that its owners were considerably under-insured. There can be no doubt that the *Titanic* casualty shocked the insurance market, just as it stunned the entire nation. *Fairplay*

at the time reported that the *Titanic* risk had been written for twelve months at a rate of 15s. per cent, describing this as "insanity". The Editor wrote that "Some . . . underwriters consider that the loss of the *Titanic* will be productive of good to the market in the long run, as it will prove to underwriters the absurdity of blindly following the lead of one company underwriter as they have done for so long at such an absurd rate as 15s. per cent, no reduction. Some of the underwriters have taken £2,000 per name, and practically all the companies have large lines on the vessel, one company having £65,000 on the hull and £20,000 on disbursements."

*Fairplay* also noted at the time that "Underwriters' sense of fairplay at the treatment in America of Mr Bruce Ismay last week found expression in a note with the signatures of all the London underwriters on the *Titanic* appended. Its terms were as follows:— 'We, the undersigned marine underwriters, desire to express to you our very sincere sympathy in the pain and loss which the disaster to the White Star Steamship Company's *Titanic* has brought to you.'

"In reply, a telegram in the following terms was received from Mr Ismay:— 'Please convey to the marine insurance companies and Lloyd's underwriters my sincere and heartfelt thanks for their kind message of sympathy, which is deeply appreciated. — BRUCE ISMAY'

"This is the first time that underwriters, smarting under a heavy loss, have addressed such a communication to the owners of the vessel lost. Their native sense of justice prompted it."

But at least one insurance company managed to escape excessive losses on the *Titanic*. At the annual meeting of the Alliance Assurance Company shortly after the loss of the White Star liner, it was reported that the company had lost some £7,000 by the *Titanic*, £5,000 on the hull and £2,000 in merchandise. *Fairplay* quoted one speaker at the meeting who said that it was "simply marvellous" to him that the "great Alliance company should have such a trivial amount of risk in one of the greatest disasters which certainly in the last thirty-four years I have known . . . There is not a little company in London which has not, I believe, something over £20,000 or £30,000 on the *Titanic*, and how Mr Ogilvie, the company's underwriter, could have steered so clear in getting such a trivial amount of risk is a mystery to me."

It was reported that the *Titanic* claim was settled within two weeks of the casualty, but this tragic loss focused still greater attention in the market on the question of inadequate levels of rating. The point had been made in 1911 that the effect of those improvements which *had* been achieved in hull rating levels was to a great extent being nullified by the increased cost of repairs. The cost of repairs continued to increase in the following year and hull insurance became even more unprofitable. During October and November, 1912, meetings were held between hull underwriters in the Lloyd's and company market which produced agreements which, it was hoped, would put business onto a more satisfactory footing.

Underwriters were doubtless glad to see the back of 1912, which had proved to be a disastrous year for hull business, and not only as a result of the *Titanic.* There were numerous other large casualties in the liner trades, among them the *Delhi,* the *Mongolia,* and the *Oravia.* Another familiar echo of present-day underwriting problems is to be found in the underwriting reports for 1912, with insurers bemoaning the fact that the 'human element' was responsible for so many casualties. One underwriter remarked at the time that the need for more adequate premiums was fully recognised but that the "application falters because hope so largely enters into the underwriters' composition."

The Joint Hull Agreement of 1912 did bring some improvement in hull rates, but many felt that premiums were perhaps still 10 per cent lower than economics should dictate. And the following year saw the Agreement dissolved when it was found necessary to exempt from further increases those fleets which were showing good results. The operations of the American Hull Agreement were also suspended, although contact was still maintained with underwriters in the United States through the I.L.U.

In 1912, a committee of company and Lloyd's underwriters and representatives of Lloyd's Insurance Brokers Association drafted eight standard clauses to be used for brokers' business, and underwriters were asked to insert in slips the words "Institute Cargo Clauses." The following "neutral" set of clauses, in which the average conditions were left to be negotiated, was issued for use from August 1, 1912:—

### INSTITUTE CARGO CLAUSES

1. Warranted free of capture, seizure and detention, and the consequences thereof or any attempt thereat, piracy excepted, and also from all consequences of hostilities or warlike operations, whether before or after declaration of war.
2. Warranted free of loss or damage by strikers, locked out workmen or persons taking part in labour disturbances or riots or civil commotions.
3. General Average and Salvage Charges payable according to Foreign Statement or per York-Antwerp Rules if in accordance with the contract of affreightment.
4. Held covered, at a premium to be arranged, in case of deviation or change of voyage or of any omission or error in the description of the interest, vessel or voyage.

5. Including (subject to the terms of the policy) all risks covered by this policy from shippers' or manufacturers' warehouse until on board the vessel, during transhipment if any, and from the vessel whilst on quays, wharves or in sheds during the ordinary course of transit until safely deposited in consignees' or other warehouse at destination named in policy.

6. Including risk of craft and/or lighter to and from the vessel. Each craft, raft and/or lighter to be deemed a separate insurance. The assured is not to be prejudiced by an agreement exempting lightermen from liability.

7. Including all liberties as per contract of affreightment. The assured is not to be prejudiced by the presence of the negligence clause and/or latent defect clause in the bills of lading and/or charter party. The seaworthiness of the vessel as between the assured and the assurers is hereby admitted.

At the same time, a set of Free of Particular Average Clauses was issued, with Clauses 1 to 7 being similar to those in the cargo clauses but with an eighth clause as follows:—

8. Warranted free from Particular Average unless the vessel or craft be stranded sunk or burnt, but the assurers are to pay the insured value of any package or packages which may be totally lost in loading, transhipment or discharge, also any loss of or damage to the interest insured which may reasonably be attributed to fire, collision or contact of the vessel and/or craft and/or conveyance with any external substance (ice included) other than water, or to discharge of cargo at a port of distress, also to pay landing, warehousing, forwarding and special charges if incurred.

In 1916, these clauses were to be reissued with Clause 1 amended to include the words "arrest, restraint" after "Seizure" in the first line and with "detention" deleted, following the decision in the case of *Sanday v British & Foreign.* This was the first amendment to the Institute Cargo Clauses. Further changes were to be formulated in 1919 but, owing to the absence of agreement with Lloyd's Underwriters' Association, the issue of the new clauses was postponed. Lloyd's underwriters required the agreement of all insurance companies to use the new clauses, and not just members of the I.L.U. The matter was duly resolved, and shortly afterwards the Institute Cargo Clauses with no Average Clause were withdrawn and the familiar Institute Cargo Clauses (W.A.) and I.C.C. (F.P.A.) came into general use throughout the world.

In the second decade of the 20th century, labour disputes began to occur in Great Britain with disturbing regularity, especially in the transport trades. In 1913, an agreement was reached by underwriters in London, Liverpool and Manchester, as well as by the Lloyd's market, not to insure liabilities for strikes expenses in any cargo policy. There was also a proposal to extend the usual strikes clause so that the warranty would include freedom of claim for expenses arising from strikes, lockouts, labour disturbances, riots and civil commotions whether incurred under a contract of affreightment or otherwise. Underwriters, whilst expressing their willingness to accept such risks under special wordings, were anxious that this additional risk should not come to be regarded as part and parcel of the normal cargo cover.

The same year saw the end of the Persian Gulf Agreement, originally made by Lloyd's and company underwriters in 1907 to cover cargo shipments on F.P.A. and W.A. conditions from the U.K./Continent to Persian Gulf. It was alleged that the reason for the Agreement being dissolved was that German underwriters took advantage of it to secure practically the whole of the business going, and at rates considerably below the tariff. It had been understood that German underwriters would support the Agreement, but it transpired instead that the British market lost almost all its outward business to the Gulf.

In the last week of July, 1914, very little marine business was being transacted in London, practically all the slips written in the market being in respect of war risk insurance. We are indebted again to *Fairplay* for the following thumbnail sketch:— "The market for war risks business is a very limited one, and the few underwriters who were entertaining the business were literally beseiged by brokers who were inundated with orders and inquiries for rates. The bulk of the business done was on goods in steamers of all nationalities to and from all parts of the world. Naturally, however, the greater part of the business done was on goods carried on vessels proceeding to and from the East via the Suez Canal, although considerable interest was shown in three or four heavy consignments of gold from the United States and the Argentine and Brazil.

"The market being so limited, it was considered desirable by the companies willing to entertain such risks to fix the rates day by day, and accordingly daily meetings were held at the Institute of London Underwriters to agree upon the minimum rates to be charged for the day. At first, Lloyd's underwriters were inclined to accept business at rates considerably under those fixed by the Institute but, as the situation became more tense and orders came pouring in, the rates fixed by the Institute became the minimum at which business could be placed at Lloyd's."

On August 4, 1914, Great Britain was at war with Germany.

ÆQUITAS ACTIONUM REGULA

34

# Chapter 4

# The Great War

So far as marine underwriters were concerned, the most obvious and immediate commercial effect of the outbreak of war was a worldwide disruption of trade. And because of the great danger to shipping arising from the war-time conditions, insurance premiums in the marine market initially received a much-needed boost. Many tariffs were increased while others were introduced for the first time.

Upon the outbreak of war, the British Government inaugurated a National War Insurance Office in accordance with a scheme already approved by the Committee of Imperial Defence. An advisory board was formed on which the I.L.U. Chairman, Mr Herbert T. Hines, accepted a seat, together with a former chairman, Mr R.B. Lemon. The war rates charged by this office were uniform and payable irrespective of voyage. From August 5 to August 7, 1914, the rate was fixed at 5 guineas per cent, then reduced to 4 guineas up to August 17, after which date regular reductions brought the rate down to a minimum of 1 guinea by the end of the year.

But the war risks office could not hold rates at this figure and, after increases to 2 guineas per cent for steamers and 4 guineas per cent for sailing vessels on December 16, 1916, rates the following year climbed to 5 guineas for steamers and 10 guineas for sailing vessels.

When in August 1914, the Government War Risks Department reduced the war rate to 2 guineas per cent, the I.L.U. arranged to reduce its rates to the East proportionately. There was a certain amount of ill-feeling between the London and Liverpool companies in this connection because it was alleged that, whilst adhering strictly to tariff rates for marine business, some of the Liverpool companies made significant concessions on their war rates, thereby securing an unfair advantage in the struggle to compete for business. Although we now live in far less troubled times, underwriters today are still sometimes accused of making surreptitious cuts in war risk rates. As in war, so too in peace . . .

The effect which the war had on marine rates sometimes evidenced itself in rather unusual ways. In 1914, for instance, it was reported that underwriters were obtaining without any trouble whatsoever such high rates as 7s.6d. per cent for coverage on F.P.A. conditions of cargo from the

U.K. to India. This was partly due to the absence from the market of competitive German underwriters, but there was another more significant reason. Shipments to India had to be covered against war risks by the State Department, and it was necessary to obtain marine policies before the war risk insurance could be effected. In the past, the Government had always been uninsured for marine risks and, since very high-value cargoes were frequently involved, the additional strain which this development placed on an already contracting insurance market had the effect of automatically forcing up marine premiums.

By the end of 1914, it was reported that the year's shipping casualties were not as serious as might have been expected considering the enormous increase in the amount of tonnage employed during the first months of the war. Nonetheless, a steady stream of what were described as 'minor casualties' were finding their way into underwriters' claims books.

During 1915, almost one-quarter of British merchant shipping was requisitioned for naval or military use, while the output from domestic yards dropped to one-third of its pre-war level. Those owners whose vessels were requisitioned or ordered by the authorities to make voyages or deviate from any route or carry cargo which would entail a breach of warranty in any policy issued by an Institute company were held covered at a rate to be agreed when details were known. In those cases where the Government assumed the risks usually covered by a marine policy, Institute companies agreed to suspend or cancel their own insurance for the period covered by the Government and to give a daily pro-rata return of premium.

The Liverpool Underwriters' Association annual report released in January 1915 included a table showing marine losses for the past five years. This put losses during 1914, including those vessels sunk by mines or cruisers, at the enormous total of £13.6m. Some £4.09m of this total was accounted for by just eleven vessels. These figures compared with those for previous years of £6.74m (1913), £6.51m (1912), £5.14m (1911), and £6.22m (1910). Largely due to war casualties, then, 1914 had produced losses which were double the average of the previous years.

At the L.U.A. meeting held in 1915 to release the Liverpool Under-writers' Association's annual report, one underwriter complained that time insurances were again "unsatisfactory" as a result of the much higher costs of labour and materials owing to the war. As a result, he said, the cost of repairs was probably 30 to 40 per cent above that of the year before. It was thought that this increase represented an additional charge of about 16 per cent on aggregate claims, so that unless hull insurance rates were increased underwriters would face a certain loss on their business.

Daily meetings of Institute underwriters, which had been a feature of the early days of the I.L.U., were resumed following the outbreak of the war, but in 1915 the frequency of such gatherings was reduced to twice each week unless special circumstances dictated otherwise. Throughout the war years, in fact, the work of the Institute went ahead despite the fact that every member of the I.L.U.'s permanent clerical staff had by the end of 1915 enlisted in the armed forces.

Early in 1915, an attempt was made to form an agreement to put hull insurance on a more satisfactory footing but, although this did come into operation, the anticipated improvement in underwriting results was, as had been foreshadowed at the Liverpool Underwriters' meeting the previous year, largely nullified by the enormous increase in repair costs in terms of labour and materials. By the end of 1915 it was apparent that further rate increases were essential if any improvement in underwriting results was to be maintained. An agreement was made that year to insert in all policies covering U.K.-registered tramp steamers the 15 per cent Disbursements Clause upon whatever terms insured. Excessive amounts placed under subsidiary insurances had long since reduced underwriters' premium income without lessening to a comparable extent their liability for average claims.

On the war front, the Germans introduced in 1915 a campaign of submarine attacks against British shipping. In May of that year the 30,396 gross ton *Lusitania* was torpedoed in an incident which resulted in appalling loss of life and which one commentator at the time described as ". . . simply the wanton act of an irresponsible people." The hull of the *Lusitania* was insured for marine risks to the tune of £800,000, and for about the same figure in respect of war risks. The vessel was entered with the Liverpool & London War Risks Association, the Government reportedly having some 80 per cent of the risk by way of reinsurance. Only a small amount of the security on the *Lusitania* was provided by the companies and Lloyd's underwriters.

Rates in respect of war risks insurance in these early years of the war continued to fluctuate more or less in concert with the latest casualty situation. In January 1915, after the Government War Risks Department had brought its rates down, underwriters in the London market were reported to be quoting in the region of 5s. per cent to Italy, for instance, with maybe an extra 2s.6d. for Egypt. India, meanwhile, was attracting rates of between 10s. and 12s.6d., and the River Plate, £1 per cent. Early in the same year, the following rates were apparently being obtained in London "to pay a total loss if peace is not declared between Great Britain and Germany on or before the following dates: June 30 — 75 guineas; September 30 — 50 guineas; December 31 — 25 guineas."

There can be little doubt that underwriters were realising profits under their war risks policies. The National War Insurance Office, of course, only covered British ships for war losses, so underwriters were able to do a

*The "Lusitania" — 'simply the wanton act
of an irresponsible people'.*

tremendous amount of business on the ships of neutral countries. It was reported at the time that the profits already secured by some of the companies and syndicates at Lloyd's had put them beyond any loss even if the Germans were successful in sinking merchant tonnage on an enormous scale.

It appears that 1916 brought little improvement in hull rating levels, and the effect of increases in the values of ships could in no way compensate underwriters for the heavy repair bills coming out of the yards at this time. One of the most striking features of the insurance business at this time was the continued increase in the value of steamers. A large number of fleets were renewed in 1916 at values which showed increases of between 50 and 100 per cent. This presented difficulties for underwriters who in many cases took a proportionate amount of the risk and were therefore compelled to accept extremely large lines.

During the war years, port congestion was obviously a serious problem to traders. In some instances, the traditional restrictions of insurance cover appeared insufficient to cope with the numerous delays in delivery and the frequent instances of carriage by unusual routes. As a result the Institute got together with Lloyd's underwriters in July 1916 to formulate an agreement whereby the words "All risks of whatever nature" were not to be included in cargo insurances and by which the risk of pilferage was only to be included upon payment of an additional premium.

Also in July, 1916, a uniform policy for signature by companies was introduced with a view to saving labour in the offices of companies and brokers, both of which were suffering from severe staff depletions. This scheme involving the joint signature of one policy by all Institute companies participating in the risk was widely used during the remainder of the war.

*The biggest sailing ship ever built — the 8,000 dwt square-rigger "France II."*

At the beginning of February, 1917, the Germans renewed their campaign of unrestricted submarine warfare. It was estimated that, by April, one ship out of every four leaving British ports never returned. During that month, nearly one million tons of shipping was lost, two-thirds of it British. Neutral ships refused cargo for British ports. New-buildings could only replace one ship in ten. But the introduction of the convoy system saved the day, and by the end of 1917 British and American yards were building almost as many ships as were being lost, although many vessels not in convoy were sunk, especially in the Mediterranean. As a result, the flat war rates which had been in force since April, 1917, were abandoned and a series of differential rates used in their place.

It was in 1917 that the Institute Committee drew attention to delays in effecting permanent repairs to vessels owing to the shortage of tonnage and of repair facilities. In many cases substantial temporary repairs were carried out at considerable cost without diminishing the cost of permanent repairs executed at a later date. The cost of labour and material had risen to a level of 130 per cent above pre-war prices, with still further increases inevitable.

At the annual meeting of the Liverpool Underwriters' Association in 1917, the Chairman, Mr Samuel Barker, made the point that war risks were much more in the nature of a gamble than were marine risks because the rates had to be "estimated in anticipation of the future" while in marine business they were fixed on the experience of the past. Noting that some of the risks covered under marine policies were more like war risks, Mr Baker said that vessels had been loaded in a way which would not be permitted in times of peace, excessive deckloads having been carried. He added that the deeper loading of shelter-deck steamers would undoubtedly result in serious deck damage, causing delay for expensive repairs. Whilst accepting that the enormous increases in ship values had helped underwriters, Mr Barker said that both marine and war risks had been out of all porportion to the premium received and that underwriters should therefore set their house in order by increasing premiums and restricting conditions of coverage.

Mr Barker was not alone that year in calling for underwriters to rethink both rates and conditions. A *Fairplay* editorial at about the same time said, "There is not the slightest doubt that underwriters will have to make special efforts to safeguard their interests in the future in many ways, especially as the premium for war risks is not likely to prove so remunerative in the future . . . There has been a growing carelessness on the part of underwriters in accepting all sorts of conditions for cargo insurance based on the fact that the additional premium for the war risk would compensate for any extraordinary losses in the marine section. Now that this possibility has to a large extent been swept away, they will be faced with heavy claims for marine risks without adequate compensation, and the sooner this has the attention the better it will be for the market. Theft claims, for example, are mounting up with rapidity, and it seems impossible to cope with the trouble, owing to the congested state of the ports. Thefts are also reported to take place on shipboard, which owners endeavour to put aside under the terms of the bill of lading.

"Although under the recent agreement the risk of pilferage has to be specially marked in the slip with the premium required, it is generally found in practice that to all intents and purposes the rate agreed for the whole risk, including pilferage, is the same rate that was charged for the marine risk alone.

"The proposed increase in rates for steamers on time is all to the good, but it must be borne in mind that conditions of trading are much more hazardous than in pre-war times. Steamers have to voyage out of the accustomed routes and incur risks which are not ordinarily taken. Another point to be considered is that the salvage companies are more or less in Government hands, and it is impossible to render prompt assistance in salving a vessel as in the past."

Underwriters were also criticised at this time for a certain amount of slackness when renewing open covers. Throughout 1916 and 1917 there had been a number of instances of underwriters having to take declarations by any old steamer at the cover rate because the wording of the slip read simply "Steamer and/or Steamers." A proper wording had still not been arrived at by the end of 1917, although the recommendation was that, for full cargoes, the wording should read "Approved Steamers or held covered", while for parcels it was thought "Liners or Steamers not more than 15 years old and classed 100 A1 or equal or held covered" would be the most suitable provision. But even with this wording there was a problem because many of the steamers declared for cargo across the Atlantic had been built on the American lakes and, although they were classed 100 A1, they were apparently not fitted for the North Atlantic, particularly in the winter months.

In 1917, the Institute companies and Lloyd's underwriters adopted an agreement to the effect that, in all cases where deferred premiums were agreed, the usual 5 per cent brokerage (but only 8 per cent discount) would be allowed in place of the 5 per cent and ten per cent discount.

The same year also saw the inauguration of an arbitration scheme in respect of missing vessels. A number of well-equipped seagoing vessels had inevitably been lost at the height of the German U-boat offensive, with little or no evidence to determine if the loss was attributable to marine or war perils. In order to avoid unnecessary delay in the settlement of such losses, an arbitration scheme was agreed between the Admiralty, the Board of Trade and the Ministry of Shipping on the one hand, and the marine insurance companies, Lloyd's underwriters and insurance clubs on the other.

A further development in 1917 was the formation of the Marine Insurance Committee, consisting of members of the I.L.U., Lloyd's, and the Liverpool and the Glasgow Underwriters' Associations. The committee's objective was to deal in an advisory capacity with legislation and other questions affecting the status of British marine insurance generally. The Institute representatives were Messrs. E.F. Nicholls, R. Lawton Tate, H.T. Hines and G. Lyall.

It was also in 1917 that Messrs. Witherby & Co. first issued in book form all the clauses then in use with the companies and with Lloyd's underwriters. The book of clauses, extremely well received at the time, retailed at a cost of 5s.

*Title page from With-erby's first "Clause Book" published in 1917 and now in its 55th edition.*

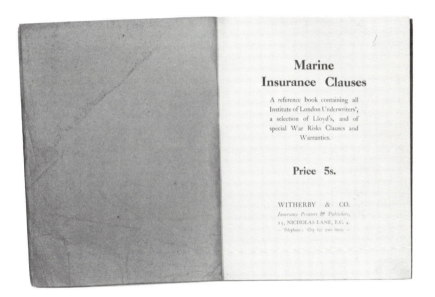

> **Marine Insurance Clauses**
>
> A reference book containing all Institute of London Underwriters', a selection of Lloyd's, and of special War Risks Clauses and Warranties.
>
> **Price 5s.**
>
> WITHERBY & CO.
> *Insurance Printers & Publishers,*
> 15, NICHOLAS LANE, E.C. 4.
> — Telephone : City 657 (two lines). —

By the early weeks of 1918, the previous year was being described as a "satisfactory" one for underwriters, despite the problems created by the war, and it was expected that all classes of business would show a profit. The Liverpool Underwriters' Association's annual report released in 1918, however, noted that cargo business had been less profitable than usual during the previous year. This was attributed in part to damage and shortage claims brought about by laxity and carelessness in handling, both in loading and discharge, which is of course still a problem for today's cargo underwriter. The same report noted that ". . . we all know that the

## A Problem Shared . . .

15 per cent disbursement clause, now universally recognised by all concerned, has been the means of underwriters obtaining a fair valuation in their policies. The adoption of this clause has helped to abolish the vicious system of excessive 'total loss only' insurance which was becoming far too general in the market."

The decision to make the 15 per cent disbursement clause available to liner tonnage had in fact resulted in an enormous increase in the values of

*The "Mauretania", 1906 — the fastest and most advanced trans-Atlantic liner of her time.*

liners as compared with previous years. Many liner owners were now insuring their fleets where previously they had elected to be uninsured, while other owners had decided to upgrade their cover from F.P.A. conditions to full terms.

The final year of the war was also marked by yet another attempt to discontinue the practice of giving 15-day returns or returns for a period of less than 30 days. The agreement drawn up this time related to all steamers registered in the U.K., whether liners or tramp steamers, including river steamers, salvage vessels, tugs, dredgers and any other form of steamer excluding cable vessels and yachts.

Also in 1918, the delay in effecting permanent repairs to vessels due to the rationing of steel and other materials and to the requisitioning of shipbuilding and repair yards, became more acute than ever. Only temporary repairs were permitted by the Government, which held shipowners responsible for the seaworthiness and efficiency of the vessel. One result of this was that the greater part of the merchant fleet was in a state of more or less bad repair, and work on the damage, particularly that in respect of machinery, was severely delayed, much to underwriters' disadvantage. By 1918, the cost of repairs had risen to somewhere between 150 and 200 per cent above pre-war levels.

At the end of 1918, Mr Edward F. Nicholls completed four years' service as chairman of the Institute, the longest term of office enjoyed by any I.L.U. chairman this century. Certainly Mr Nicholls appears to have been an extremely able and active man, being in addition to his I.L.U. offices a member of the War Committee of the Chamber of Commerce and of the Insurance Advisory Committee on Recruiting, as well as being on the committee of Lloyd's Registry of Shipping. Sadly, his health appeared to have suffered as a result of his exertions, and he vacated the chairmanship of the Institute in 1918 to take up a seat on its committee.

He was to return to the chairmanship in 1926, but one suspects he must have found things by that time comparatively dull. When the armistice was signed on November 11, 1918, he had seen the I.L.U. successfully survive the war years, despite enormous difficulties. Indeed, it might be said to have more than survived, its membership having risen from the 1913 level of 33 companies to a figure of 47 in 1918. Now it had to prepare to face the problems of peace and what American President, Warren Harding, described in 1921, as the need for "normalcy."

AEQUITAS ACTIONUM REGULA

46

# Chapter 5

# *Between Wars*

THOSE Institute members who might have hoped that the cessation of general hostilities in 1918 would lead to a return to normal life were quickly disappointed. Marine underwriters were in fact about to embark on a period which was to prove far more difficult in many respects than the troubled years of the First World War. The loss during the war of a tremendous amount of shipping, followed by a worldwide demand for goods of every description, resulted in a significant increase in both hull values and in the price of those commodities carried as cargo. Although this for a time produced an increase in premium income, other factors greatly outweighed any advantage which might have accrued to underwriters from this source. During and immediately following World War One, various extraneous risks were first widely underwritten in the market as insurers, against a background of rock-bottom cargo war rates, began writing extremely wide terms of coverage in an attempt to compete forcefully for any business on offer. Also at this time, the cargo market was hit by an epidemic of losses by theft, pilferage and short-delivery, while there was a spate too of cases involving the deliberate scuttling of merchant tonnage. To make matters worse, repair costs by 1919 were estimated to be 250 per cent above pre-war levels.

So far as problems in the cargo market were concerned, the Institute and Lloyd's underwriters agreed early in 1920 to limit liability for theft, pilferage and short-delivery to 75 per cent of the insured value of any goods so lost. But this was destined to be a short-lived agreement, full cover being restored the following year as the efforts to reduce pilferage were seized upon by some underwriters as an excuse to make concessions on rates and conditions.

The hull market, meanwhile, was exhibiting similar signs of recovery and relapse. The immediate post-war boom attended by increased premiums was followed quickly by a drop in insured values and the entry into lay-up of large numbers of ships. Despite numerous efforts to reach some form of agreement on hull insurance, that part of the Joint Hull Agreement dealing with hull rates and values had been suspended by the middle of 1921, it being impossible to operate in a climate of dramatically falling hull values.

## A Problem Shared . . .

But some attempt was made to control the situation. The Institute Time Clauses, for instance, were reissued with the Disbursements Clause limiting disbursements and freight to 10 per cent and 15 per cent respectively in place of the previous 15 and 25 per cent of the hull and machinery value.

It is doubtful if any section of the commercial community faced the future in the early 1920s with more trepidation than the shipowners. Many owners had bought vessels, often with borrowed money, at the end of the war at inflated prices. And as ship values began to fall, hull underwriters were presented with a large number of total loss claims. Some vessels were said to have struck drifting mines, some were destroyed by fire while others unaccountably foundered.

*Forerunner of a popular modern concept — the 1921-built heavy-lift vessel "Belfri" with a cargo of locomotives.*

It was noticeable, however, that these vessels were lost in fine weather, in water too deep for divers to examine the wrecks, and close either to land or to regular shipping routes. And although the casualties were occurring with disturbing frequency, very few lives were being lost, which is generally something of a 'give-away' in this regard. (Even today, the accounts of some alleged scuttlings make interesting reading with their descriptions of crew members abandoning sinking tankers with their personal possessions neatly packed in suitcases and their freshly-cut sandwiches and their flasks of coffee in hand).

A further curious circumstance was noticed by underwriters at the time. Almost all the losses involved vessels flying the Greek or Spanish flag, and all were insured for amounts far in excess of their true values. In February, 1921, Lloyd's and company underwriters attended a joint meeting and appointed a committee to enquire into all suspicious instances and agreed to withhold settlement of pending claims until the committee reported its findings. The committee, under the chairmanship of Mr E. Griggs of the Merchants Marine Insurance Company, acted with the London Salvage Association under the direction of Sir Joseph Lowrey. Expert investigators were engaged to examine each suspicious casualty. Observers of today's insurance market will doubtless be struck by the similarities between this 1921 initiative and that undertaken many years later by the aptly-named FERIT (Far East Regional Investigation Team).

At a further meeting of interested underwriters back in 1921, the proposal for continued non-settlement of suspicious claims in the absence of complete enquiries was approved, each case thereafter being considered on its merits. Those claims found to be free from suspicion were promptly settled. Of the others, some were settled by compromise at amounts ranging from 15 per cent to 90 per cent of the insured value, a few claims were dropped by assureds, and the remainder were resisted in the courts. The great majority of the court cases were won by underwriters.

The records show that Capt. F.W.S. Mogg of the Salvage Association (who was later to gain official recognition for his valuable work in the face of great difficulties and dangers) investigated no less than 38 cases involving insurances of over £3m.

The years immediately following the end of World War One found the companies and Lloyd's underwriters in rather an embarrassing position as a result of their declaration some years earlier not to allow any hostilities between Britain and Germany to affect the fulfillment of any liabilities of British underwriters to German assureds. (See Chapter Three). A statement, signed jointly by the Chairman of the Institute of London Underwriters and the Chairman of Lloyd's, was eventually issued in August, 1921, explaining that, although British underwriters had agreed that their policies would be fully valid for marine and war risks (including British capture where covered), the signing of the Treaty of Peace with Germany at Versailles in 1919 had entirely altered the situation.

The statement noted that "The Agreement is not one-sided; just as German assureds have agreed in the terms of the Treaty (of Versailles) that they will not make claims upon British insurers for loss by British capture, so have British assureds and reassureds agreed that they will not make claims upon German insurers for loss by German capture. And the assureds of both nations would seem equally bound by their agreement in honour as they are in law . . ."

## A Problem Shared . . .

The statement concluded with the comment that "British underwriters . . . desire to put on record . . . their decision to carry out the terms of the Treaty as imposed upon them by both the German and British Governments. Those German assureds who have suffered through the agreement of their Government on this point might be held to have a grievance against their Government and possibly to be morally entitled to compensation from them; but no grievance would appear to be against the English underwriters."

Meanwhile, the everyday problems of the market continued apace and, in 1924, important amendments were made to the conditions for both hull and cargo insurance. The most significant change so far as the hull market was concerned was the insistence by underwriters on the use of the Institute Time Clauses without alteration for liners or tramps of whatever flag, unless it had been the custom in the past to grant the owners special clauses or, in the case of foreign vessels, recognised national conditions. It was also agreed that new insurances other than those made on special owners' conditions or recognised national conditions would be subject to the Institute Time Clauses unaltered. This represented a great advance on the confusion of clauses in existence some thirty years previously.

*Tokyo in ruins following the Japanese earthquake in 1923 — the Joint Hull Committee appointed a representative to go to Japan to supervise huge claims which fell on the market in the wake of the disaster.*

In the cargo market, the spate of post-war scuttlings finally proved to be the motivation behind an amendment to the Bill of Lading Clause in the Institute Cargo Clauses to protect innocent assureds. Also in 1924, the Warehouse to Warehouse Clause was revised in an attempt to define more clearly the limits of cover. On an infinitely sadder note, the year also saw frequent meetings of a special Joint Committee convened after the Japan earthquake the previous year which had left Tokyo and Yokohama in ruins and, in the process, presented the Institute companies with some huge claims. Sir Joseph Lowery found further expression for his special talents in this unhappy arena also, being appointed by the Joint Committee to go to Japan to supervise the examination and certification of claims.

Another important development in the cargo market took place in 1924 when the Institute executive entered into discussions with a number of trade associations with a view to drafting mutually acceptable insurance conditions for a variety of commodities. The first fruit of this liaison was the publication at the beginning of 1925 of the Flour All Risks Clauses, as agreed by the National Association of Flour Importers and the Institute of London Underwriters. The same year also saw the publication of an amended set of Institute Strikes Risk Clauses and the first appearance (following Government concern over the illicit trade in opium and other drugs) of the Institute Dangerous Drugs Clause.

These were difficult years for marine underwriters, and a clue to the mood of the industry can be gained from a speech given by the Institute chairman in 1925. Mr H.T. Hines said that "Prevailing conditions have produced competition of the most severe type, and under these circumstances the duty of protecting the basic and fundamental principles and safeguards of marine insurance has entailed very heavy work and much anxiety. Even shipowners agree that present rates are below cost." How many shipowners, one wonders, would be prepared to make such an admission today?

A new Joint Committee which was destined to play a significant role in the affairs of the London marine insurance market was inaugurated in 1925. The Technical & Clauses Committee, consisting of representatives of the London and Liverpool companies and Lloyd's underwriters, first met on January 28, 1925. Among the clauses issued during its first year of operation were the Institute Yacht Clauses and the Institute Yacht Protection & Indemnity Clauses.

By 1926, the year of the General Strike (from which marine insurers appear to have escaped very lightly in terms of damage claims) there had been a slight improvement in hull insurance. During the previous year, certain company underwriters had come to a private understanding with regard to renewals, and the Joint Hull Committee recommended that this

## A Problem Shared . . .

Understanding should receive the support of both company and Lloyd's underwriters. The support was widely given and, as a result, it seemed that there might be some improvement in hull insurance results, albeit a marginal one at first. In the following year, a general increase of 10 per cent on most hull insurances continued the slow and hesitating movement towards profitability. Market leaders said that shipowners had not raised serious objections to the surcharge because "for many years they have been buying their insurance below cost." Despite the increase in rates, however, the high cost of repairs was not always taken into account, with the result that further rate increases were still needed if hull business was to become profitable.

By the time the 1926 renewal season came around, it was generally accepted that the Understanding had proved its worth. While cargo insurance appeared to be going from bad to worse, with inadequate rates (50 per cent less than those of 1921 according to some sources) and over-generous conditions very much the order of the day, hull risks were showing encouraging signs of being written on rates and conditions which bore some relation to the state of the market.

But hull business was still a long way from being a profitable concern and those underwriters assessing renewal figures for 1928 would have had to have taken account of a spate of shipboard fires which hit the market in the previous year. During a three-month period that year, there was a serious shipboard fire almost every other day. The Liverpool Under-writers' Association made special mention of the number of unexplained fires at sea in its annual report, and the Board of Trade undertook special research in connection with shipboard fires in general and fires in coal cargoes in particular. Here again we have a perfect example of how certain problems continue to find expression throughout the history of the marine insurance industry. Subscribers to the Mississippi coal cargo insurances and on the slips of the numerous vessels which were lost and damaged through fires and explosions in the early 1980s, will find nothing new in the problems experienced by their 1927 counterparts.

In 1928, most Institute companies moved office, either to the new Lloyd's building in Leadenhall Street or to premises close by, although the offices of the Institute itself were to remain at St Michael's House until September 1930, when they moved to 37/39 Lime Street. But if 1928 brought a change of address for many companies, it did nothing to dilute in any way the sense of the wider moral obligations which the Institute had always felt was an essential part of its constitution. What was seen by one commentator at the time as a "work of social benefit" took place in 1928 when the Institute decided not to insure consignments of arms and munitions bound for the various warring factions in China which, following the fall of the Manchu dynasty and the collapse of the

Republican regime, was in a state of virtual anarchy. The Institute suggested to kindred associations throughout the world that they might adopt a similar approach to that taken by the I.L.U. and Lloyd's, and as a result the agreement was signed by most marine insurance markets.

Any prospect for the overall profitability of marine underwriting was at this time extremely thin. Despite the comparative success of the Hull Understanding, rates were still too low and it was said that underwriters were helping shipowners to operate their vessels by providing them with extremely cheap insurance. In 1929, the I.L.U. Chairman said, in a speech which could have (and indeed *has*) been echoed by many of his successors, that "No trade can succeed if it cuts its own throat by excessive philanthropy." In the same year, at least one Institute company dismissed staff as a result of the distinctly unpromising outlook for marine business.

So far as cargo business was concerned, the trend towards low rates and extremely wide coverage was carried forward from the 1920s into the next decade. One I.L.U. man uttered the disturbingly familiar words that ". . . The inclusion of war . . . risks without additional premium . . . is particularly ill-advised" and that rates were ". . . hardly sufficient to pay for the extraneous risks, and nothing is left for the major casualties that must inevitably occur from time to time."

In 1930 (a year in which the London market was confronted with a number of heavy Greek losses instead of the mass exodus of Greek tonnage to a new Greek Insurance Pool which had been threatened) the Institute chairman said that the Joint Hull Committee was "trying to save the market from itself." But by the end of that year, reductions had been generally allowed in hull values without any increase in rating levels.

By this time, merchant tonnage was becoming bigger and more sophisticated. Plans had been proposed to build a large and luxurious passenger liner, and the first steps taken to construct the vessel which would eventually be launched as the *Queen Mary*. The British Government, considering that the value of this vessel would be beyond the capacity of the marine insurance market, duly passed the Cunard Insurance (Agreement) Act, but was heavily criticised for taking such action without consulting the Institute or underwriters at Lloyd's.

This Government decision led to insurance terms being offered for the construction risk which were considered by a number of underwriters to be unsatisfactory. It was made clear in Parliament that neither the rate fixed for the main risk nor the terms for continuation were considered adequate. Those insurers who objected were pilloried by publicity given to the names of companies who had written the risk and also by appeals to the patriotism of the reluctant underwriters. In the end, insurance to the tune of £2.7m was placed in the market, the balance of £1.8m being covered by the Government. But work on the vessel was suspended towards the end of 1931.

**A Problem Shared . . .**

*In the 1920s a steam engine was a familiar, if tricky, cargo to handle — and cargo insurance rates were going from bad to worse.*

The early 1930s were in fact marked by a series of terrible fires in passenger liners, and the I.L.U. chairman was in 1932 co-opted onto a committee of shipowners, shipbuilders and underwriters which examined this phenomenon. Beginning with the constructive total loss of the *Bermuda,* 1932 saw the loss of the *Georges Philippar* and the *Pieter Cornelius Hooft,* followed in 1933 by *L'Atlantique,* and in 1934 by the *Morro Castle.* In later years, too, the market was to be hit by the loss of the *Layfayette* and the *Paris.*

Referring to the *L'Atlantique, Fairplay* commented in January 1933 that "It is a matter for surprise that the Minister of Merchant Marine in France has issued a series of new and stringent regulations to be observed by French liners carrying passengers before the result of the inquiry as to the cause of the fire on *L'Atlantique* has been ascertained . . . Strange to say, I can see no provision for the use of fire-proof wood for the cabin bulkheads in the French regulations. It states that wooden panelling for gangways and passages must be protected by asbestos, but the only provision for living quarters is that the ceiling must be of non-flammable metal. Provision is made for the control of the ventilating system from a central point, but it would be interesting to know how it is proposed to control the draught in the lift-shafts and the stairways. In large passenger

*The "Queen Mary" — government action without consultation with underwriters.*

*The "Morro Castle"*
*beached off New Jersey*
*in 1934 — the early*
*1930s were marked by*
*a series of terrible fires*
*in passenger liners.*

steamers the keynote is one of continual vigilance, so that the outbreak may be located and suppressed without delay. One good point about the new French regulations is that on steamers of more than 15,000 tons gross, three professional firemen should be carried, while on vessels accomodating more than 250 passengers there should be a fire-fighting squad of three to six men who have had a period of training with professional firemen."

Throughout the late 1920s and the early 1930s, the Hull Understanding had been a steadying influence on the market at a time of cut-throat competition in other sectors of the business. But in January 1933 the Joint Hull Committee allowed the "Respecting the Lead" agreement to lapse. The brokers blamed the 'leaders' for the collapse of the agreement, while others blamed the brokers themselves. One commentator remarked at the time that ". . . The market is back again to the position it was in twelve years ago. Will history repeat itself? Will certain underwriters who like to see their initials at the head of a slip fall for the deft and disinterested flattery of the brokers? Or will underwriters who take over a lead make quite sure that they have got all the figures necessary for their guidance?" Whether they did or not, it does seem that, after the abandonment of the agreement, the majority of renewals were placed on reduced values and rates, and this was by no means in all cases a concession given in return for good results.

## A Problem Shared . . .

At about this time, the extent of war risks cover was occupying a good deal of the Institute's time. War risks cover had been included in marine policies since the First World War. By the 1930s, the war risk was being included without extra premium and subject to ten days' notice which, as one critic observed at the time, was worthless from underwriters' point of view because, if war were to break out anywhere, underwriters were on all the risks bound to the areas of conflict, while future shipments would cease. They could fix additional premiums but nothing would come in, so that they had all the war risks on their books for no premium at all.

By 1934, cover was being given for long periods before loading and after discharge, and underwriters eventually became anxious to limit the periods during which war risks cover would apply under marine policies. A series of negotiations ensued thereafter without a mutually acceptable solution being found, before Lloyd's and company underwriters decided on September 16, 1935, in view of the existing international situation, to give the requisite notice under all contracts. It was further agreed to hold the assured covered at the expiry of this notice provided the request for cover was received prior to such expiry.

*A dramatic picture of the French liner "L'Atlantique" ablaze in 1933 — 'no provision for the use of fireproof wood.'*

Subsequently, a Rating Committee, representative of both company and Lloyd's underwriters, was appointed to formulate agreed rates for open covers and policies, such rates to be day-to-day rates for immediate shipments, *i.e.* sailings within seven days from receipt of enquiry but subject to immediate acceptance of the rates.

The first schedule of rates drawn up by this committee was issued on September 25, 1935, and amended schedules were issued from time to time thereafter, the particulars of which were notified by cablegram or airmail to kindred associations. The Rating Committee continued to issue schedules of minimum war and strikes rates and, during 1936, Lloyd's and company underwriters adopted agreements regarding the writing of war and strikes risks.

On the marine side, 1936 also brought an important development in connection with the processing of risks. In a year in which the Institute noted in its annual report the death of King George V and the accession of George VI but studiously avoided any reference to the recently abdicated Edward VIII, fundamental changes were made to the method of closing marine insurances. In order to simplify the work of both brokers and underwriters, a closing slip of standard form and size was adopted by Institute members, this at a time when individual company policies were still in general use.

By 1937, the hull market had begun to find the absence of concerted action in the wake of the demise of the "Respecting the Lead" agreement too much to bear and the possible short-term profits of a completely competitive market less and less likely to materialise. A number of important agreements were thereafter adopted, the first being the Hull Understanding of March, 1937, dealing with the question of rates on vessels whose values were increased during the currency of the policy and providing that no reduction might be granted on renewal.

There followed in the ensuing months, and indeed up to the outbreak of World War Two, a number of further agreements aimed at improving hull business, this at a time when ship values were continually being increased, vessels were being taken out of lay-up and either employed on commercial business or filled with scrap metal cargoes and delivered to Japan and other countries to be broken up and thereupon remade into warships, munitions and other artefacts of war.

The War Risks Rating Committee met frequently to consider revisions of the schedule of war and strikes rates during the early part of 1938, a year which also saw the introduction of the Waterborne Agreement restricting war risks coverage to periods whilst waterborne. These meetings were prompted generally by the uncertain international situation and especially by the Spanish Civil War and the Sino-Japanese conflict.

## A Problem Shared . . .

In September, 1938, the War Risks Rating Committee was in almost constant session until the 'accord' reached between Chamberlain and Hitler appeared to have averted the European crisis. The telegram sent to Prime Minister Chamberlain on September 30 was, like many others of the time, rather unfortunately worded, but it is only with the benefit of hindsight that we are able so to describe it. It read: "On behalf of the members of the Institute of London Underwriters I hasten to send you our heartfelt congratulations on the success which has attended your efforts. You have earned the gratitude of all mankind. A.M. RICHARDSON (Chairman) INSTITUTE OF LONDON UNDERWRITERS."

On October 6, 1938, the Editor of *Fairplay* wrote that "It was rather astounding to learn on Friday last week that, after the war cloud had lifted, some firms, amongst them important and responsible concerns, had requested a reduction in the rates to which they had previously agreed when the war scare was at its height. Friday's temporary scale of war risk rates was specifically stated "Not to apply to risks declared previous to September 30" and it is, of course, established law and practice that, once a rate has been fixed and accepted there can be no variation made because the circumstances affecting the risk have changed after the rate was fixed. There must still be quite a lot of cargo passing through the Mediterranean insured at the rate of 2s.6d. per cent, fixed by Schedule No. 31, which was the last general schedule to be issued before rating by the War Risks Rating Committee temporarily ceased on September 13. Would the assured who enjoyed protection at that rate have considered any application from underwriters for a further £4.17s.6d. per cent at the time when the Mediterranean rate stood at £5 per cent last week? I hear that one merchant, in attempting to cover the war risk on some shipments on a steamer, stipulated that, in the event of no war being declared, he should have the whole of the premium returned including, apparently, the brokerage. Unfortunately for him, no underwriter would write the risk with such conditions. The risk was afterwards placed, and the unfortunate merchant has now lost the whole of his premiums, owing, I suppose he would say, to the greed of the underwriters."

In the same issue, *Fairplay's* Editor also had a word to say about the I.L.U. He wrote that "I do not think the passing of the crisis should be allowed to fade in memory without some tribute being paid in print to the work of the Institute of London Underwriters during the difficult days of the past three weeks. No doubt other underwriting and kindred institutions also did magnificent work during that period, but on the Institute fell the whole task of preparing and issuing the schedules of rates compiled by the Joint War Risks Rating Committee, and this was but a fraction of the work that had to be carried out at a time of exceptional stress. It must be remembered that the Institute was in daily touch with foreign and other underwriting institutions, that even during the utmost press of recent times there was a great deal of routine work to be carried out and that, from the very nature of its functions, the Institute was the body to which all turned for official information at a time when it was essential that such information should be accurate and quickly available. I think the market owes a debt of deep gratitude to Mr H.E. Gordon and his staff."

On September 15, 1938, prior to the Munich Agreement and following a market meeting of underwriters, notice had been given to cancel the provision for the inclusion of war risks in all insurances and it was agreed that at the expiry of this notice all war risks must be covered separately in the market. Later, on October 13, it was decided that provision for war risks might be reinstated in marine covers, subject to a 48 hour cancellation clause.

Members of the Institute and other insurers found themselves in a difficult position with regard to war risks insurance. Some such cover was necessary if trade was to continue, and only underwriters at that time could give this protection for cargo and specie. War rates ruling in September 1938 would not have been adequate if a major conflict had broken out. Swift action was necessary and notice was given of the cancellation of war risks under covers because the market could not agree on new scales and it was not certain that assureds would have accepted them.

But at no time was the market closed to the writing of war risks. As the I.L.U. Chairman later explained, it was evident within 24 hours that underwriters and assureds required and would follow a revised scale and the Committee almost immediately functioned.

Scales of rates were periodically issued, each giving a reduction on those previously in force, until by January 1939 it was said that except for long-distance voyages, rates were at about the same level as those in force the previous September. The Munich crisis illustrated the difficult position in which war risk insurers so often find themselves. If war does break out, then underwriters may suffer huge losses, but if there should be no war after serious threats, they are accused of profiteering.

On April 13, 1939, a special pool, as advocated by the I.L.U. Chairman and named the War Risks Cargo Pool Management Ltd., was formed. All premium in connection with war risk insurances on voyages to or from the United Kingdom had to be paid to this pool irrespective of whether the business was written in the U.K. or through agencies in other countries.

Thereafter, international events took their inevitable course and war broke out on September 3, 1939. There was to be no reprieve this time. The Institute, now with a 76-strong membership, was about to adapt for the second time in its history to the peculiar needs of a world at war.

ÆQUITAS ACTIONUM REGULA

# Chapter 6

# *The Second World War*

UPON the outbreak of the Second World War, many Institute companies secured office accommodation outside London in an attempt to minimise the disruption of business by air raids. But the smooth running of the companies was inevitably interrupted by staff depletions upon the mobilisation of the volunteer forces and then by the regular conscription of others according to age and the essential nature of their employment within their respective offices.

One of the first administrative changes brought about by the war was the introduction in November 1939 of combined policy forms for use by all Institute companies. The use of these forms, which were processed by Lloyd's Policy Signing Office with the help of company employees, greatly facilitated closing procedures at a time when the limited number of staff would obviously have struggled to cope with the processing of a multitude of individual company policies.

Another change which was quickly introduced upon the outbreak of war was the formation of the so-called "Eighteen Company Group" whereby eighteen companies combined to form one underwriting syndicate with two underwriters on duty on a rota basis. But this was so unpopular with the brokers that it was abandoned after only one month of operation.

By the end of 1939, cargo insurance was in an extremely bad way. The poor state of the business was made critical by the outbreak of war and the inevitability of further heavy losses. In the first few months of hostilities, cargo underwriters were confronted with several large losses attributable entirely to the war, and it was clearly absurd that cargo insurance rates should remain at their depressed levels. But the problem for underwriters was that many annual covers had already been renewed and, despite the appalling losses, the market was still too weak for any corrective measures to be enforced.

An idea circulated at this time for an agreement to "Respect the Lead" to be inserted in cargo policies apparently met with stoic indifference in the market, the general feeling being that cargo business did not lend itself to agreements of this nature in the way that hull insurance did. But a new development was just around the corner.

## A Problem Shared . . .

A scale of surcharges was adopted by company and Lloyd's underwriters on January 18, 1940, applicable to all cargo and specie insurances for voyages in certain defined combat areas, while on September 1 of the same year the surcharges were increased and the area extended. On May 20, underwriters had agreed to charge an additional premium on all shipments, whether by liners or tramps and whether insured W.A. or F.P.A., via the Cape from the United Kingdom to Egypt, Persian Gulf, India and the Far East and vice versa. On October 24, the agreement was extended by the fixing of an additional premium on shipments via the Cape and Port Said from the U.K. to Mediterranean or Black Sea destinations and vice versa.

The incisiveness and adaptability which underwriters had shown during the First World War was quickly in evidence again during World War Two. When Norway was invaded in April, 1940, all insurance policies became automatically ineffective and, at the request of the British Government and in order to secure Norwegian tonnage for the Allies, arrangements had been made in the market within 24 hours to underwrite the whole fleet, the value of which was colossal.

On a more prosaic note, meanwhile, hull insurers in 1940 continued to give support to the Hull Understandings. In January a revised agreement was adopted providing, *inter alia,* for an increase of 25 per cent after the application of the percentage increase payable according to the credit balance over the past four completed years. In August, the Joint Hull Committee considered the position of vessels soon to be submitted for renewal and which at the time of their previous renewal had been subject to the surcharge of 10 per cent called for by the Understanding of September 15, 1939, apart from any increase for poor results. The Committee decided that where the 10 per cent had previously been charged, a minimum surcharge of 15 per cent could be applied on renewal in addition to any increase called for by the application of the Understanding.

The scales of additional premiums for cancelling various of the Institute Warranties were increased by 25 per cent from August 1, while returns of premium for various eventualities were also matters considered by the Joint Hull Committee at this time. A number of vessels had been requisitioned by the Government, which provided the equivalent of insurance cover whereupon underwriters suspended their own insurances. A clause was drafted which provided that no claim would be recoverable under the marine policy during the period of requisition and that returns of premium for that period would be payable in accordance with the recommendations of the Joint Hull Committee.

Laying-up returns were at the time subject to change, for in all insurances under the Institute Time Clauses or Standard Dutch Hull

Form written after October 1, 1940, the premium retained by under-writers for a vessel laid up in port was increased to 18s. per cent per annum if laid up in the U.K. not under repair or, if abroad, 30s. per cent per annum. Later it was decided that on insurances placed subject to owners' clauses, which were still used for liner fleets at the time, the retention would be increased by not less than 50 per cent, as would all insurances effected on limited terms.

In the same year, a new and more equitable method of levying subscriptions to the Institute was adopted, based on a flat subscription plus an additional levy on net premium income as shown in the member's balance sheet. A fund subscribed by company and Lloyd's underwriters was set up at about this time under the title "Underwriters' Recovery Fund" for use in taking legal action in neutral ports against German shipowners to obtain the release of British cargo detained in such ports. Transfers were made from this account to a "Cargo Owners' and Underwriters' Legal Fund". The funds were in the nature of loans, payments therefrom being reimbursed by payments collected from cargo owners. Out of this Under-writers' Recovery Fund an amount was set aside to meet the costs of taking to the House of Lords certain test cases in connection with cargo in German vessels.

At about this time, many company underwriters availed themselves of an invitation from the Committee of Lloyd's to use the underground shelter facilities in the Lloyd's building. When the air raid siren was sounded, company staff working in offices in the building would gather up their essential papers and, following the complicated coloured signs on the walls of the corridors, make their way to the basement where they would set up temporary underwriting areas until the All Clear was sounded.

1940 also saw the beginning of the Food and Supply Insurance Scheme, whereby a contract was made between company and Lloyd's underwriters and the Ministry of Food and Supply for the insurance of all shipments for account of the Ministry. A committee of management was formed under the chairmanship of Mr G.A.T. Darby, Marine Insurance Co., to fix rates, handle claims and supervise the running of the scheme.

One of the many problems which the war was causing at this time was the loss of overseas documents as a result of enemy action. In the case of the loss of bankers' drafts, this caused serious delays in the remittances reaching their proper destination and resulted also in considerable expense to the parties concerned. Arrangements were accordingly made for the adoption by company underwriters and the banks of a mail transfer system whereby the banks, for payments in Britain, agreed to accept a specially worded Insurance Companies' Scheme form instead of purchasing drafts in connection with United States and Canadian Dollar transactions.

## A Problem Shared . . .

Although by 1941 a large proportion of United Kingdom imports were insured under the Food and Supply Master Slip, there was still a great deal of cargo insurance rated by leading underwriters, who were reminded by the Institute to quote adequate rates in line with the Surcharge Agreement. There seemed to be little doubt that cargo underwriters were undermining the market by offering injudiciously low rates and expansive coverage.

At about this time, too, concern was expressed in connection with the liabilities which some underwriters had assumed by reason of excessive amounts covered at any one location. It was recommended that the Location Clause in open covers should not exceed 100 per cent of the cover limit per bottom, or at most 200 per cent, considerably below the 400 and even 500 per cent which had been granted on a number of covers at that time.

Although the outbreak of the war had predictably produced a more cohesive hull insurance market, there was still much room for improvement in hull rates. The cost of claims settlements had increased substantially during the war years with a good deal of unrepaired damage waiting to be attended to at a future date, doubtless at greatly inflated prices.

The war also gave rise to the need in certain cases to formulate special hull underwriting agreements. For instance, following the Axis invasions of Yugoslavia and Greece, arrangements were made for the insurance of vessels from these countries which had been requisitioned by their respective governments. Although the policies on these ships had become invalid, a form of endorsement was framed whereby in return for a nominal premium the policies were reissued.

There was certainly no shortage of technical work for the Institute in 1941. Another matter which gave rise to concern was the status of Government-owned vessels under open covers where the rates differed according to liner or tramp ownership and to age and tonnage. A formula was duly agreed whereby the term 'Liners' was held to include vessels operated by British liner owners on behalf of the Government if they had previously been owned by regular, foreign liner fleets and were not over twenty years old or more than 5,000 gross tons and were classed 100 A1 or equivalent. Also included in the 'liner' description were vessels built after 1939 of 5,000 gross tons or over and classed 100 A1 or equivalent.

Also in 1941 the Returns Bureau introduced an amendment in connection with the examination of claims for laying-up returns on certain foreign vessel insurances. Policies were stamped with the notation "Facts Agreed. Joint Hull Committee Returns Bureau", and any claims for returns of premium might thereafter not legally be paid or, if their legality was in doubt, a licence was required from the Trading with the Enemy Branch (Treasury and Board of Trade) prior to payment.

But perhaps the most significant event in the marine insurance market in 1941 was the formulation by the I.L.U. and Lloyd's Underwriters' Association, at the request of the United States Maritime Commission, of an advisory scale of additional premiums for use in connection with insurances under open covers which included the classification clause, limiting the age of the carrying vessels on voyages between the United States and the U.K. to "not over 20 years". The scale was as follows:

|  | Metals all risks; other interests, F.P.A. Per cent | With average but hazardous interests h/c Per cent |
|---|---|---|
| Age | s.d. | s.d. |
| 21-25 years ................ | 1.3. | 2.6. |
| 26-30 years ................ | 2.0. | 4.0. |
| 31-35 years ................ | 3.4. | 5.6. |
| 36-40 years ................ | 5.0. | 7.6. |
| Over 40 years ............. | 7.6. | 10.0. |

This was described at the time as the first known occasion on which there had been direct collaboration between underwriters and a foreign Government department.

Whatever else their problems may have been, underwriters were not lacking in business during these difficult years. Notice was given in January 1942 that Lloyd's and the company offices would be open for business on Saturdays. This, in fact, represented a *return* to Saturday working which had been suspended during the early years of the war when it had proved difficult for staff to arrive on time in a day when the actual underwriting hours were of necessity limited.

The Joint Hull Understandings were amended again in January 1942 to allow renewals on fleets which had complied with previous Understandings to be completed at existing rates unless the credit balance over the previous three completed years was considered inadequate. In November of the same year a further amendment was introduced to the effect that "This ruling only applies to increases after the policy has been in operation for a period of three months . . ."

At about this time, a disturbing anomaly arose as a result of the wartime conditions. As in many cases the insured values of hulls fell short of replacement valuations, many owners elected to collect a claim for 100 per cent partial loss, as opposed to a constructive total loss, and to retain the vessel. On occasion, owners would also claim a total loss under the disbursements policies. As a result, the Total Loss and Excess Liabilities Clauses were amended to make it clear that, should a vessel become a constructive total loss but the claim under the hull and machinery policies be settled as a partial loss, no payment would be made for total loss under the disbursements policy. It was also stipulated that should a claim for total or constructive total loss be settled on the hull policies as a compromised total loss, the amount on account of disbursements would be the same percentage of the sum insured as that paid on the hull policies.

Perhaps the major event of 1942 in the marine insurance market was the formulation of a clause aimed at providing a clearer dividing line between marine and war risks and removing some of the anomalies in the operation of the Free of Capture & Seizure Clause. The new clause, to be used for all new business and in all war risk policies as they expired, transferred to the marine policy certain additional hazards such as stranding when avoiding enemy attack, collision where both vessels were to blame even though one was engaged in warlike operations, and collision with a war vessel even though it might be alone to blame.

The famous *Coxwold* judgement of 1942 (*Yorkshire Dale Steamship Co. Ltd. v Ministry of War Transport*) was of the utmost significance so far as the revision of the F.C. and S. Clause was concerned. The *Coxwold* was in a convoy of four ships engaged in a 'warlike' operation under the command of a naval officer. During her passage, a change of course was ordered owing to the close proximity of an enemy submarine; subsequently, under the influence of an unexplained tidal set, the *Coxwold* stranded. It was held by the courts that the loss was 'a consequence of a warlike operation' and as, a result, underwriters of marine insurance were rather surprised to discover that they were not liable. After the decision in this case, the marine insurance market's conception of what constituted a war loss was radically altered.

A Wartime Extension Clause supplemental to the Institute Cargo Clauses was also published in 1942, providing for delay, deviation and other eventualities caused by wartime conditions. A schedule of minimum, obligatory supplementary rates, subject to the terms of the Extension Clause, was drawn up for approved cargoes and amended from time to time, the rates being subject to 15 days' notice of cancellation.

War risks business was transacted under rates largely governed by the Advisory Schedules. The system appeared to operate smoothly, although some anxiety arose in the market over one incident in July 1942 when the War Risks Insurance Office announced that the Overseas Schedule, which had previously only applied to cargo in British ships, would be extended to include cargo in Allied and neutral vessels. It was feared that this extension of the Government scheme would diminish the volume of business on offer in the commercial market, but assurances were given that it was not the intention to compete with the open market in the overseas trade but only to provide facilities for such trade when those of the commercial market proved inadequate.

At this stage of the war, much of the Institute's effort was directed towards minimising the workload of a severely depleted workforce. One of the first fruits of these endeavours was the adoption in March 1942 of the Three Leading Underwriters Agreement which provided that, subject to brokers undertaking to give reasonably prompt advice to underwriters of minor agreements initialled by the three leading company underwriters on a slip, such agreements would be binding for all company underwriters on the risk.

Another example of this desire to streamline the rather thin wartime resources of the Institute found expression in October 1942 when, under the superintendency of Mr W.H. Ridley, who later became Manager and Secretary of the Institute, the I.L.U. opened its own Policy Department to deal with the issuing of combined policies and the checking of additional premiums and returns. No longer would company policies need to be processed at Lloyd's Policy Signing Office, which had been of tremendous help to the Institute in the past. The new facility quickly proved its worth, a total of 272,000 combined policies being issued in 1942 as against the estimated 1.36m individual company policies which would have had to have been signed. *Fairplay* noted that the creation of the I.L.U. Policy Department was "a wartime measure perhaps, but one likely to become as much a permanency as Lloyd's Policy Signing Office which was, in its initial form, a labour-saving device of the last war." Prophetic words!

1943 produced yet another wartime and time-saving innovation when, in an effort to expedite the settlement of claims submitted by brokers, a special procedure was introduced by which the full claims papers were shown only to the leading companies, all other insurers receiving from the brokers forms merely outlining the claim. Those underwriters requiring more information could arrange to see the claims documents if they so wished. This system proved so advantageous that, although introduced as a merely wartime expedient, it continued until being superceded by the introduction of similar forms issued by the Institute.

The same year saw a major change in the cargo insurance market in the form of the introduction by the I.L.U. and Lloyd's Underwriters' Association of the Combined Marine Surcharge. This was a new comprehensive addendum to the basic rating of marine cargo risks, aimed at embodying in a single charge the various additional charges in the cost of marine insurance arising out of war conditions at sea. First among the charges was a tariffed additional rate superimposed upon the basic marine rate to offset the increased perils of navigation due to war conditions. Next in chronological order were the additional premiums on certain voyages to the Eastern Mediterranean and Near East paid for deviation via the Cape on voyages which would normally be made via the Straits of Gibraltar. Finally there was an additional premium for the Institute Cargo Clauses (Wartime Extension) which had previously been optional and dependent on the election of the assured to obtain, for an initial premium, cover against deviation, delay, transhipment and other variations of adventure due to wartime conditions. The new Combined Marine Surcharge also contained provision for "the additional cover granted by the amendment of the British F.C. & S. Clause", but this appeared to be more in the nature of a token premium than an actual charge.

The underlying idea of the new schedule was that, in place of separate additions to the basic marine rate, there should be a compulsory surcharge embodying all these in one comprehensive rate. It was thought that the average cost of cargo insurance as a result of the introduction of the C.M.S. would probably by no greater than before, while those who had previously elected to insure under the Wartime Extension Clauses would now actually pay much less.

1943 also brought an amendment to the Waterborne Agreement permitting unlimited transhipment cover. The effect of this change was to enable the assured to obtain continuous war risks cover at ports of transhipment even if the period of 15 days after arrival, to which cover was limited by the Institute War Clauses, was exceeded. It was expected that the banks and financial houses, interested in cargo by reason of money advanced on maritime adventures, would especially appreciate the greater security afforded by this amendment. Insurers, meanwhile, were quick to point out that the permission to cover an unlimited period during transhipment did not offend against the basic principle of the agreement and that it had been given in response to a very real need, which American underwriters had already recognised, since they had been giving unlimited transhipment cover in certain trades for some time before British underwriters took this decision.

In the Autumn of 1944, the Joint Hull Committee decided to renew the Understandings without alteration. The outlook for hull underwriting by this time was in fact very uncertain because the amount of unrepaired damage had not diminished and the cost of repairs, which had already risen so dramatically, was almost certain to climb even higher as a result of the introduction of measures to protect the well-being of shipyard workers. Underwriters were also greatly concerned at this time about the prospect of delayed repairs and at the realisation that so much repair work on British ships was being carried out under lease-lend agreements in the United States, with the likely result that the final repair bill would probably not be presented to the owners until possibly two years after the completion of repairs.

*The Grant of Arms
to the I.L.U.*

The generally improved conditions of 1944 brought about a reduction in the Combined Marine Surcharge. Those areas in which the reductions were less than general were those in which there had been a recurrence of the theft and pilferage problems that had prevailed during and after the First World War. Much of this increase in pilferage was a direct result of the inferior packaging in use because of wartime conditions. This, coupled with the increase in demand for stolen goods supplied by the large body of 'spivs' to otherwise respectable purchasers in consequence of the severe rationing of goods and the operation of the 'coupon' system, was of course in no way the fault of the shippers. For this reason, the 75 per cent theft and pilferage clause which had been so effective after 1918 could not fairly be reintroduced on this occasion.

# A Problem Shared . . .

The Armorial Bearings
of the
INSTITUTE OF LONDON UNDERWRITERS.

College of Arms
London. 14 July 1943.

A. T. Butler
Windsor Herald.

In June 1943, the Institute was granted and assigned the following Armorial Bearings:-
ARMS — Argent, a cross gules, between in the first and fourth quarters a galley sable, on water barry wavy proper, and in the second and third quarters a lighthouse upon a rock, all also proper.
CREST — A sea-lion proper, supporting with the fins a fouled anchor sable.
The motto adopted by the Institute was Aequitas Actionum Regular ("Let equity be the rule of our actions".)

Speaking of cargo premiums at the time, *Fairplay's* Editor wrote that "I imagine that many underwriters' cargo statistics over the period of the war are, on paper, looking entirely satisfactory, but one must remember that there are very few underwriters who, despite the shortage of staff, are able to devote the time to separating war premiums from purely marine risks, and I have little doubt that, if this was done by an underwriter who is in the habit of writing a general cargo account, there would be a rude awakening."

A decision was taken at the end of 1944 at a special general meeting of the I.L.U. which was to have a significant effect on the Institute's future method of operation. It was resolved that the Articles of Association should be amended by the insertion of a clause permitting the Institute to appoint agents in any part of the world to settle claims as agents for and on behalf of members of the Institute, and to pay claims by means of drafts upon, or otherwise out of the funds of the Institute but only if the insurers on whose behalf the claim had been settled should previously have agreed with the Institute to repay the money so provided. This represented a significant addition to the scope of the I.L.U.'s activities and added to its international standing in the ports of the world.

With the end of the war in 1945, it was time once again for taking stock of the underwriting position in the marine market. In its issue of May 17, 1945, *Fairplay* commented that "Peace has come to Europe, and it is permissible to say that the marine insurance market has emerged from the war years with prestige enhanced and security undiminished."

On reflection, it could be said that the stout maintenance of the Joint Hull Understanding had been of great service to underwriters in very difficult circumstances, and that the loyalty with which the market had supported the Joint Hull Committee was evidence of the valuable work it had undertaken. So far as cargo insurance was concerned, its history during the latter years of the war had been inexorably bound up with that of the Combined Marine Surcharge and the Food and Supply Open Cover, and it was noticeable how the rates had been substantially reduced with the general improvement in the war at sea. The cost of war risks insurance, too, had fallen in concert with the increasing likelihood of an Allied victory, and in April 1945 market war risk rates were brought into alignment with those of the War Risks Insurance Office, so ending a period of virtual Government monopoly of UK war risks business.

Not surprisingly, the war had necessitated a number of clause amendments and rating revisions, and the end of the hostilities brought a general expectation that there would be an overhauling of marine insurance clauses and a fear that rates would be cut back substantially now that the fighting had ceased.

Mr. E.F. Nicholls, Institute Chairman from 1915 to 1918, had noted in reference to the First World War ". . . how wonderfully all the underwriters of the companies of London supported everything that the Government wished done, and in that connection I feel very grateful to the members of the Institute for the fact that if I went up to a Government department and they wished underwriters to do such a thing, I did not have to give underwriters any reason. They said 'If the Government wishes it done, do it!'"

Mr. C.E.P. Taylor, Chairman in 1944, said that history had repeated itself and that he was sure that the (then) present generation of Government officials, no less than their predecessors, had learnt that they could always look to the members of the Institute for wholehearted co-operation in difficult times such as those through which they had recently passed.

AEQUITAS ACTIONUM REGULA

74

# Chapter 7

# Post-War Years

By the end of 1945, things were slowly returning to normal at the Institute, whose membership by now numbered 89 companies. The I.L.U. Committee had welcomed the decision of the Government to bring marine insurance within the ambit of the Assurance Companies Act and to take steps to prevent the formation of companies on a basis that was not financially sound. Even more welcome had been the statement by Sir Stafford Cripps in November 1945 when moving the Second Reading of the Assurance Companies Bill that the Government had no intention of interfering with the free transaction of marine insurance by private enterprise. Sadly, this was not an example followed throughout the world, and the post-war years were marked by an obvious increase in nationalism in many countries which greatly affected the freedom of marine insurance. This problem has grown considerably in more recent years, and there are now an unprecedented number of governments which operate restrictive legislation affecting the freedom to place marine insurance contracts.

But business had to go on as usual, whatever the international situation. During 1946, the Institute's Articles of Association were extended to comprise vessels, aircraft, cargoes, freight or other objects of marine, aviation and transit insurance. Two new and extremely important (if diverse) paragraphs were at the same time added to the Articles, one giving the Institute the power to appoint agents in any part of the world for the settlement of claims under I.L.U. Claims Payable Abroad policies, and the other giving it authority to establish pension funds and to provide money for charitable objects.

So far as hull business was concerned, 1946 saw an amendment to the Hull Understandings which provided that, where the existing rate was obtained by the application of the formula of September 25, 1945, the rate would be the existing rate corrected according to the formula for results. However, if the rate had been obtained by the application of the formula previously in use, the new rate would first be reduced in accordance with the September 1945 formula and then corrected according to the formula for results, thus continuing to grant the assured the benefit of the 1945 general rate reduction.

Meanwhile, repair costs continued to cause concern in marine insurance circles. They had obviously risen during the war years, and in 1946 the I.L.U. Chairman estimated that costs had risen by between 100 and 150 per cent compared with levels obtaining in September 1939. In times of war and peace, prosperity and hardship, the rise in repair costs seems consistently to have mitigated against any lasting profitability in hull underwriting.

Cargo underwriters at this time were still accruing some much-needed additional premium from the application of the Combined Marine Surcharges, which continued to operate alongside those strictly tariff rates which had survived the disruptive war years. There were those who argued that the justification for the existence of the Combined Marine Surcharges had disappeared with the ending of the war, but the truth was that the additional hazards had merely changed in *character* now that the fighting had stopped. Theft and pilferage losses, for example, were at this time rampant throughout the world, with such commodities as piece goods and textiles a favourite target for the villains.

These were the years of the 'spiv', who was to be seen in his long, waisted overcoat (arguably with ladies' nylons hanging out of the pockets) standing on the edge of bomb-sites selling goods of all descriptions but universally doubtful origin.

In July 1947, the Combined Marine Surcharges were revised, a zone system being introduced with just two sets of rates — one for F.P.A. or W.A. conditions and the other for approved cargo on fuller conditions. For non-approved cargoes on fuller conditions, the amount of surcharge was left to underwriters' discretion. After two world wars, the cargo market had finally come to accept the need to give wider coverage than W.A. conditions on non-approved cargoes.

On a general note, it was becoming apparent at this time that, despite the spread of nationalism which characterised the operation of the marine insurance industry, many of the small local markets could not safely or profitably retain their own business. As a result, steps were taken to offer these surplus proportions through reinsurance treaties to other insurers, including Institute companies. The Institute Policy Department provided the facilities for dealing with such treaties but of course had no responsibility for the terms of any individual treaty, the inadequacy of retained lines and the magnitude of deductions from ceded premiums being a matter for those underwriters who accepted such business.

This growth of treaties from countries where Institute members were hampered on every side in their efforts to set up or continue to maintain agencies and branches was a phenomenon much criticised by some members. The critics' viewpoint was expressed succinctly in *Fairplay* on October 30, 1947, when the Editor wrote that "Surely a market which prides itself on individual choice is giving up its birthright when it largely

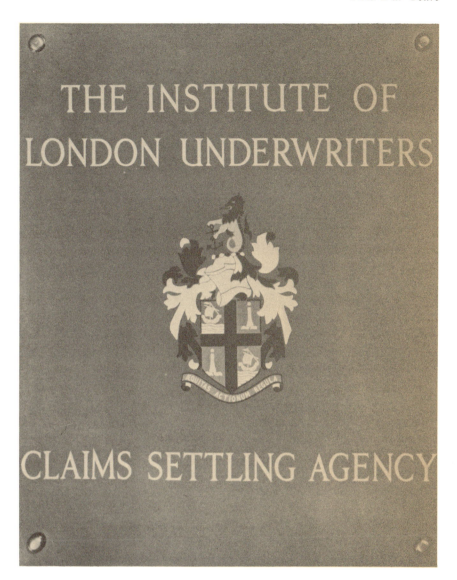

THE INSTITUTE OF
LONDON UNDERWRITERS

CLAIMS SETTLING AGENCY

*1944 saw the first steps taken towards appointing ILU agents in ports throughout the world.*

subscribes to risks, the terms of which it has repeatedly condemned individually, but is not strong enough to refuse or amend collectively.''

Treaty reinsurance had been a part of insurance practice for many years prior to the close of the Second World War but the prime motive of the older treaties had been the more secure and advantageous operation of insurance and had not been born out of the nationalistic financial policies of those countries from which such treaties originated. The Institute, as was its duty, provided facilities for dealing with these contracts on a quarterly or other agreed basis, but their acceptability was a matter for individual members who differed very strongly on this question. The Treaty Section of the Policy Department had been opened in October 1945 and by 1947 it was checking the monthly or quarterly accounts of almost 300 treaties.

In the direct market, hull underwriters in March 1947 adopted a revised formula for results under the Joint Hull Understandings. The previous formula was renewed but with the proviso that, where the credit balance was 50 per cent or more, renewals might be effected with a 50 per cent rate reduction. But this reduction was withdrawn the following year when amendments were introduced to provide slightly higher rates for risks where the credit balance was unsatisfactory.

An important development in terms of the Institute's international standing had taken place in 1944 when steps were first taken to appoint agents in each port to settle claims on Companies' Combined Policies on behalf of all subscribing companies. A Book of Instructions to Agents was also prepared and issued to appointed agents, who by 1948 numbered in excess of 200.

Also in 1948, the seal of the Institute Policy Department was affixed to all Institute Companies Combined Policies. It was emphasised that when an Institute policy had been issued, no member of a company's staff could initial or overstamp any alterations, which could only be made by an agreement initialled by the companies and then submitted with the policy to the Institute Policy Department for alteration. This instruction took a number of years to really filter through to the staff of all brokers' offices, who would sometimes try to obtain an initial by a member of the leading company's underwriting room to an amendment improperly made to the policy form.

On an administrative note, it was decided in 1949 that new members elected to fill vacancies caused by retirements from membership should in future pay an entrance fee of £500 and that, if the facilities of the Policy Department were required, an additional fee of £200 would be payable. The Articles of Association at this time provided for only 100 members and, since the Institute's membership now exceeded that figure, new members could only be considered on the resignation of others. Although

*Chairman's Badge of Office, presented to the I.L.U. by the Irish Institute of Marine Underwriters in 1949.*

## A Problem Shared . . .

the Articles could not be amended to enlarge the membership due to the great difficulties of obtaining more staff and renting additional accommodation, two companies were in fact re-elected in 1950, so raising the membership to a total of 102.

The I.L.U.'s annual report for 1949 (a year in which the Institute was presented with a chairman's badge of office by the Irish Institute of Marine Underwriters) contained what to some must have been a rather surprising item of casualty news. It was revealed that, from the end of the war until December 31, 1949, no less than 74 total losses and 127 damage claims had been presented as a result of contact with mines. The worst year was 1947 (20 total losses and 25 damaged vessels) but even in 1949, some four years after the end of the war, four vessels were lost and 22 damaged from such causes.

During the post-war years, the long run-off period for claims continued to be a problem. One leading company underwriter produced figures in 1949 to show that in the seven years prior to the outbreak of World War Two there had been an average settlement after three years of 5½ per cent. But for the years 1940, 1941 and 1942 the figure after three years had climbed to 23 per cent.

The devaluation of Sterling and other currencies in 1949 also had an adverse effect on hull insurance, with British hulls and vessels of other countries whose currencies had been devalued paying over 40 per cent more in claims on costs incurred in countries not affected by devaluation. This, combined with various other negative factors, made the outlook for hull insurance look very bleak at the time.

Also in 1949, the Combined Marine Surcharges were merged with basic cargo rates. This move back to the underwriting of individual accounts according to their merits was in many respects inevitable and was welcomed by most Institute underwriters who thought that the constant stream of theft and pilferage claims would prevent any general reductions in cargo rates. But this thinking proved to be a little wide of the mark because, by the following year, competition had indeed forced cargo rates down.

This drop in rates, which was not helped by a slight improvement in the theft and pilferage situation, was accompanied by increasing demands for ever more comprehensive cover, in many cases motivated by the uninformed stipulations imposed by merchant banks financing cargo transactions. And it was this pressure to widen the scope of cargo coverage which eventually gave rise to the publication of the Institute All Risks Clauses.

Demands for wider coverage were of course nothing new, and the following year saw the spotlight switch to another familiar problem for marine insurers. At the Paris meeting of the International Chamber of

Commerce in April 1950, Mr A.W. Green noted on behalf of the Institute of London Underwriters and Liverpool Underwriters' Association that insurers were strongly opposed to the practice of shipowners accepting Letters of Indemnity in exchange for clean bills of lading. This led to a revision by the I.C.C. of the relevant section of the Uniform Customs and Practice for Commercial Credits, a move which was applauded by underwriters. Sadly, the pressures of trade and commerce are such that the problem was to recur time and again in the years ahead, and is indeed still very much in evidence today.

The question of shipowners' liability for loss or damage to cargo under the Hague Rules was also discussed during the year and, following negotiations between British shipowners and cargo and insurance interests, an agreement was promulgated on August 1, 1950 making certain amendments to the limit of value for each package, the extension of the statutory period for commencement of legal proceedings and the provision that all disputes be settled in the United Kingdom. The negotiations were conducted under the auspicies of the British Maritime Law Association and the Institute was represented on the subcommittee by Mr G.T. Charles, Mr H.B. Edmunds and Mr C.A. Stevens. A memorandum embodying the main features of the agreement was duly issued by the Institute and the Liverpool Underwriters' Association.

Meanwhile, the everyday business of processing marine insurance policies went ahead at an ever increasing rate. By 1950, the Institute Policy Department was having to cope with a heavy increase in workload in all its departments, and a punched card system utilizing tabulators was introduced to record the daily entries of each company and to prepare the companies' summaries and Claims Payable Abroad dollar accounts.

By the early 1950s there was a great deal of interest in the safe carriage and delivery of cargo. Whilst of the opinion that such matters were primarily the concern of the assured, some underwriters with Institute companies joined together with their colleagues in Liverpool and at Lloyd's to make representations to various authorities in connection with cargo loss and damage arising from the lamentable condition of certain West African ports. Quite what effect this had is uncertain but it does appear with the benefit of hindsight that the problems encountered by underwriters in this regard in the 1950s would almost have been welcomed by their more sorely pressed colleagues of the 1970s and 1980s.

At any rate, the expected drop in theft and pilferage claims after the war as a result of improved packaging, better port control and policing did not materialise. Indeed, it is probably only the advent of containerisation which in the long term has led to an improvement in the situation today.

In 1953, the so-called 'Red Clauses', which indicated to consignees the positive action they should take in the event of loss of or damage to goods, were reissued in stronger terms in order to impress more fully upon consignees the nature of the action to be taken. While one version provided for a survey report issued by Lloyd's Agents (even though a request for settlement be made to the settling agents of the I.L.U.) and another version contained no such reference to an Institute agent, two subsequent versions provided for notice to be given and a survey report obtained from the I.L.U. agent named in the clause.

Another question considered by members of the Institute at this time was the growing trend towards the continuation of cover without additional premium after cargo had been discharged from the oversea vessel. While there was a consensus of opinion among underwriters that there should be a time-limit provided in the clauses for such cover, it was reluctantly admitted that the market was not strong enough to insist upon clauses so amended and that the most that could be achieved was the recommendation of the I.L.U. Chairman that additional premiums should be charged for the worst destinations. In addition to the more usual risks of theft and pilferage and fire, 1953 brought disastrous floods both in the United Kingdom and on the Continent to add to the hazards faced by cargo underwriters at this time.

The economic difficulties flowing largely from the troubled international situation in the early 1950s were causing problems for hull insurers. The ever-increasing cost of repairs was made worse still by the requirements of Government rearmament programmes brought about by the growing aggression of the Communist powers both in the Far East and in Europe. Most shipyards were at this time so occupied with shipbuilding that they were not interested in quoting for repair work except on very profitable terms. Shortage of supplies also added to the delays with the result that the cost of materials was increased and served to add to the difficulty of assessing what would be an adequate premium to meet claims settled several years ahead. In view of this, a general surcharge of 10 per cent plus any increases demanded by the results of any ownerships was imposed on all renewals after February 22, 1951. But after a year this surcharge was dropped, despite the fact that repair costs continued to rise as a result of the increase in steel prices and wages. The surcharge was not repeated because the market was apparently reluctant to impose it on shipowners for two consecutive years since most owners had made substantial increases in the insured values of their vessels and the Joint Hull Committee considered that it would be harsh to impose again a charge on owners with an excellent record, preferring instead to rely on the "penalties in the Understanding" where adverse results had been experienced.

However, on March 11, 1953, amended scales of penalties for unsatisfactory figures were issued by the Joint Hull Committee. Together with these penalties (which were somewhat less onerous than the previous formulae) the main feature of the new Understandings was the imposition of a general 10 per cent rise in rates. Unfortunately, on October 28 the same year it was agreed by the Joint Hull Committee that the 10 per cent rise should no longer remain as part of the Joint Hull Understandings.

This was a blow to members of the Institute and indeed to all British underwriters even though the March surcharge had come as a surprise to many. However, the new Understandings appeared to be operating successfully and in September at the International Union of Marine Insurance Conference the chairman of the Joint Hull Committee had strongly defended the surcharge. He had explained that it was introduced to meet the rise in repair costs and he quoted examples of statements by shipowners deploring the continued increase in costs of both material and labour. Certainly these were significant factors, and Mr Gerald Nabarro M.P., a well known and flamboyant member of the House of Commons, remarked in the House at the time that "there has been no comparable increase in the cost of production in any manufactured article in post-war years."

At the same I.U.M.I. conference in 1953, the Joint Hull Chairman referred also to the steep rise in claims in 1951 and 1952 and said that ". . . It is in our favour that we still have a hull agreement . . ."

Shortly after the leading figures in the British market had returned from the I.U.M.I. meeting, the market was generally startled to learn that Norwegian underwriters were offering renewal on Norwegian-flag ships without the imposition of the 10 per cent surcharge. Since practically all Norwegian hulls attached from January 1 each year, such insurances were only being renewed after October 1, by which time numerous British and other national fleets had been renewed after accepting the surcharge.

British shipowners were naturally indignant. It seems that the London market was not prepared to lose its large Norwegian hull portfolio and therefore waived its surcharge for Norwegian business, but when the news became public there was a great deal of ill-feeling in the market. It was subsequently agreed that, at the next renewal, sympathetic consideration would be given to an amelioration in all instances where the March 1953 surcharge had been paid. But hull underwriting results certainly justified the imposition of the surcharge and the action of Norwegian underwriters in offering renewal without including it was much to the disadvantage of Institute members and other British underwriters — and doubtless in the long run to Norwegian underwriters themselves.

At the end of 1953, one of the Institute's great personalities retired. Mr Hugh E. Gordon, Manager and Secretary, relinquished his duties on the grounds of ill health. He had served the Institute for 43 years, 23 of them as Secretary after succeeding Mr E.P. Hudson in that post in 1930. He was regarded as a vital link between the members of the I.L.U. and the various market underwriting associations, and in 1954, in recognition of his work for the insurance market and for promoting friendly relations between the London company market and other marine insurance markets throughout the world, he was appointed an officer of the Order of the British Empire.

Mr Gordon's O.B.E. came at a time when the international marine insurance market had, generally speaking, become too large for the amount of business available. This is of course a perennial problem and one which is particularly noticeable when marine casualties are considerably below normal levels. In order to maintain or increase premium income, underwriters have tended where possible to write lines of a size which in former days would not have been considered prudent when compared with the insurers' premium income. Following this trend, other and smaller lines are swept up by a small part of the market, thus leading to more and more competition and the temptation in some quarters to reduce rates to a level that would bring heavy losses upon those who participated in such rate-cutting.

Another method of reducing premium which became popular in the 1950s was the incorporation of large deductions into reinsurance contracts. At a time when rates were being reduced to an absolute minimum, it was perhaps strange that one Institute Chairman should find it necessary to comment upon this practice and the fact that deductions were often given on the evidence of misleading figures.

But despite the apparent difficulties of making an underwriting profit in the marine market, the middle 1950s produced many applications for I.L.U. membership from companies of various nationalities. As one of the objects of the Institute was to promote, advance and protect the interests of its members, the committee at this time found itself in an embarrasing position. It was thought that the market was already big enough and that, if Institute membership was expanded, competition would be keener than ever, signing lines would be down, profit margins would be smaller and, with the spiral of inflation, management expenses would increase greatly. This was the view then held by many leading members of the I.L.U. and one which appeared to change only some fifteen or so years later when circumstances seemed to warrant it.

The low level of casualties during much of the 1950s led a number of observers to conclude that modern navigation aids and improved methods in the design and construction of ships were already resulting in a diminution of claims for loss or damage and that underwriters could well pursue a policy of progressive rating reductions. Fortunately, the general support given by underwriters at this time to the Joint Hull Under-standings prevented any landslide in rates. Shipowners had been asking for automatic reductions for good results and had been supported by some underwriters. One I.L.U. Chairman in the 1950s pointed out that while consideration could be given to the reduction of rates for good results after taking into account the problem of increasing repair costs, the introduction of a formula that provided continuous reductions based solely on claims experience would be quite contrary to the basic function of insurance unless provision was made for a minimum rate. He considered that the complexity of hull All Risks insurance was such that it was quite impractical to fix a minimum rate and that it was therefore essential that reductions in rating should be determined by a committee taking into consideration the circumstances of each insurance.

At about this time, some further examples of the results of delayed claims were published by a leading I.L.U. underwriter. The settlement of his 1946 account was 8 per cent worse at the end of its eighth year than had been the settlement of his 1945 account at the end of its eighth year. The 1947 account at the end of its seventh year was 7 per cent worse than the 1946 account at the end of a similar period. The 1948 account was better by 7 per cent when compared with that of 1947 by the end of the sixth year, but worse by 8 per cent than the settlement against the 1945 account. This apparently regular worsening of hull claims settlements added support to the argument that the introduction of an automatic reduction of rates for claims experience would indeed be difficult at a time when there appeared to be such instability in the pattern of claims settlements.

This thinking was perhaps reflected in the development in March 1956 whereby the Joint Hull Formula was amended to provide that, where the figures for the current year were such that when added to the figures for the four completed years a loss was shown, the appropriate penalty increases would be paid forthwith.

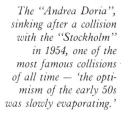

*The "Andrea Doria", sinking after a collision with the "Stockholm" in 1954, one of the most famous collisions of all time — 'the optimism of the early 50s was slowly evaporating.'*

## A Problem Shared . . .

After several years of comparatively good casualty experience, 1956 produced more than the normal number of losses. The outstanding casualty involved the sinking of the liner *Andrea Doria* after collision with the *Stockholm*. The optimism of the early 1950s was slowly evaporating, and not solely as a consequence of these expensive casualties. The Suez crisis of 1956 saw the Canal blocked and shipping thereafter forced to take the much longer route around the Cape of Good Hope. The British Government asked Lloyd's Register to extend the period for special survey for a further year over the existing one-year grace period and, since many owners did not effect damage repairs until after special surveys had been carried out, it seemed inevitable that delayed claims would increase again, which was particularly regrettable since this problem had recently improved quite noticeably. In addition, of course, underwriters also expected to encounter greater casualties arising from the longer voyages from Europe to the oil ports in the Persian Gulf, India, the Far East and Australia.

While hull underwriters were pondering the likely effect of these developments, important changes were taking place in connection with cargo insurance clauses. In 1954, the Technical and Clauses Committee had set to work amending the multitude of individual meat clauses, in the process reducing them in number from thirty-five to four. This might be seen as one of the very first attempts at the simplification of documents. In February 1956 the Joint Cargo Committee under the chairmanship of Mr Lloyd Owen introduced a 60-day limitation to the period of cover after discharge granted under the Institute Cargo Clauses (Extended Cover). This in fact stands out as a quite remarkable achievement, since cargo underwriters throughout the history of marine insurance have been pressed to grant ever wider conditions of coverage and have usually done so. This was one occasion, however, when underwriters clearly felt that "enough was enough."

The workload of the Institute was increasing all the time and on the very last day of 1956 the registered office of the I.L.U. moved to its present address at 40 Lime Street, thus enabling all departments to be accommodated in one building for the first time since 1940. The plan for these offices was drawn up by Mr George Coles, who also advised the Institute on many points in connection with office design and planning.

Hull underwriters continued to have their problems in the latter half of the 1950s. In September, 1957, the Joint Hull Committee took steps to deal with the effects of falling hull values and inflated repair costs by producing new and increased formulae for application to renewals which were readily adopted by the market. But they did not fully address the problems of the time. Ship values had been increasing since 1952, substantially so since the Suez crisis, but during the worldwide trade

## A Problem Shared . . .

recession in 1958 values dropped rapidly. Consequently, in June of that year, the Joint Hull Committee recommended that the then current formulae relating to adjustments of premium for reductions in value (which caused underwriters to refund part of the premium charged for 'average' purposes) could no longer be justified. The newly approved formulae for adjustment of premium for reductions in value provided that the calculation should be made on the Total Loss rate only.

The end of the 1950s saw both hull and cargo underwriters faced with some familiar problems. In 1959, some 3m gross tons of pre-war and war-built tonnage went to the breakers' yards. About 45m gross tons of

*One of the world's great ocean liners — P&O's 45,000-ton "Canberra".*

pre-1945 vintage was still afloat, although an appreciable amount of it comprised part of the estimated 8 per cent of world tonnage laid up at this time. Orders for new ships had fallen in comparison with the 1957 figures and shipping values were naturally below their 1957 peak. War-built tonnage was by now proving increasingly uneconomic to operate and expensive to repair as well as susceptible to both hull and machinery damage. The casualty record seemed to Institute members of the time to be showing some improvement, although a number of explosions and breakdowns in enginerooms resulted in expensive damage and heavy repair bills. As the 1950s ended there were changes to be met within the types of ship coming off the slipways. Large specialised ore carriers were carrying heavy bulk cargo from relatively unknown waters, while the growing size of bulk cargo carriers, both tankers and others, was producing problems for underwriters that would require elucidation in the years ahead.

Even so, the Joint Hull Formula for correction of renewal premiums based on results was reduced in July 1959, a step which reflected the more stable economic factors that members of the I.L.U. and other underwriters considered to be operating at that time.

At the end of the decade, the world merchant fleet totalled some 130m tons, of which 41m tons (or 32 per cent) consisted of tankers. During the same period, as an example of the capacity of the market, one underwriter pointed out that cover for the *Oriana* and *Canberra*, valued at £15m and £16m respectively, had stretched the market to the full.

*The "Amoco Cadiz" — potentially the most expensive marine disaster of all time.*

Major casualties to large tankers were by this time beginning to loom as large in the public eye as had once those suffered by passenger liners. Of the larger casualties that occurred at this time, considerable attention was paid to explosions in boiler rooms and machinery spaces, and collisions and strandings continued to take place despite the fact that many ships were by now equipped with all available modern safety devices and navigational aids. Some commentators at the time suggested that these navigation aids were contributing to "radar assisted" collisions and that the more complex machinery of modern vessels produced more engineroom breakdowns than did the old reciprocating engines of earlier days. Members of the Institute at this time must have looked at their books and noted that no improvement had taken place, either in the amount of unrepaired damage or in the unknown costs of repairs waiting to be claimed, since the criticisms voiced by earlier generations of underwriters on these very subjects.

So far as the cargo market was concerned, the end of the decade brought one particular change in emphasis. The I.L.U. Chairman in 1959 pointed out that, while some of his predecessors had spoken severely about the loss of sound underwriting principles, it was now unfortunately impossible to return to former terms and conditions. A merchant who had enjoyed All Risks cover for many years would not be content with F.P.A. insurance and, provided the results were good and the rates adequate to provide for major casualties as well as for the erosion of smaller claims, he could not be expected to accept a reduction in cover. Although this was the position in practice for a number of years, it had not been so clearly stated before as an expression of what might be termed the "new age of underwriting." Wider insurance terms and the larger proportion of business from overseas placed under reinsurance treaties were both signs of the changes in markets at home and abroad and of a weaker market in London in some respects than had been the position before.

On an administrative level, the early years of the 1960s saw some important changes taking place at the Institute. The introduction in January 1958 on an optional basis of a premium accounting scheme had been a natural progression of the successful operation of the I.L.U.'s Policy Department. In May 1960 the Committee agreed, in principle, to a Central Accounting Scheme and to negotiations being commenced on the subject with representatives of Lloyd's Insurance Brokers Association. It was not, however, until 1962 that agreement was reached with the brokers on the setting up of a Joint Committee.

The first meeting of the Sub-Committee took place in July of that year, one of the principle conditions being that there should be no contribution by brokers to the cost of the scheme. Frequent meetings ensued in a cordial atmosphere and by August 1963 work had progressed to a point where it was possible to place the proposed Scheme before Members. The Member of the Institute's staff involved throughout the whole of the project was Bernard Curtis (who at that time was Superintendent — Mechanisation and now is the Institute's Chief Executive). Unfortunately, he was on holiday when the scheme was placed before Institute members on 27th August, 1963 but the following letter was sent to him by the then Chief Executive, W.H. Ridley:—

"I know you have been wondering this morning what has happened at the "Weekly Meeting" so let me give you the news that the scheme has gone through with one or two minor details to be queried. With that news I hope you will entirely forget Central Accounting and enjoy the rest of your holiday, but before closing I must say how much I have appreciated the extreme amount of work which you have put in. Well done!"

The Sub-Committee was empowered to finalise negotiations with Lloyd's Insurance Brokers Association and the Institute Central Accounting designed to meet the needs of member companies and the brokers with whom they transacted business was finally introduced on a balance of account basis.

A milestone in the Institute's history had thus been achieved.

The early years of the 1960s ushered in a period of great change in social ideas and their application. The Vietnam War seemed to serve as a sort of ignition point for violence and disorder in other parts of the world and, whilst this might not appear at first sight to be of particular concern to underwriters of marine insurance, the hi-jacking of aircraft, destruction of buildings and widespread terrorist activity undoubtedly affected the industry in a number of ways. Acts of piracy became a very real possibility, while for those I.L.U. members writing aviation insurance the risk of aircraft hi-jackings and the question of the social desirability of ransom insurance were matters of genuine concern.

So far as the more conventional activities of the market were concerned, the 1960s began on a high note, with major casualties for the previous underwriting year unusually good. But the latter part of 1960 produced sufficient heavy casualties, followed by others in 1961 to ensure that underwriting results would again fall below average. The profit margin for hull underwriting had become so slender that no more than a few major casualties were needed to transform a profitable account into a loss-maker.

The causes of loss during the early 1960s had a disturbingly familiar ring to them. A number of newly-built vessels were lost, many as a result of collisions and strandings which, despite the use of radar and other modern navigational aids, seemed to be as prevalent as ever. Explosions in enginerooms also continued to occur with disturbing frequency, giving rise to suggestions in more than one instance that negligence was a significant contributory factor.

*Innovative vessel designs such as the 1972-built "Doctor Lykes", the world's first SEAVEE class intermodal carrier, continue to make demands on underwriting ingenuity.*

*Disaster for the aviation market — Dawson's Field, Amman, 1970.*

*Great Yarmouth, UK. Boxed fish is discharged
from drifters, a scene sadly changed today.*

Cargo underwriters in London at this time may well have been feeling rather disappointed at the failure of Britain to gain entry into the European Common Market, since they anticipated (perhaps rather optimistically) that this development would be the source of additional premium income. They must, on the other hand, have been encouraged by the support received from other national markets for the publication in 1963 losses had risen to a post-war record of 148 vessels aggregating some 517,000 tons.

At what appears to have been the first officially arranged Press conference following an Institute annual general meeting, the I.L.U. chairman Mr L.A. Locke quoted in 1964 the Liverpool Underwriters' Association figures showing how in each year from 1955 to 1958 there had been a loss figure of between 250,000 and 300,000 tons (rising all the time) but how in 1963 losses had arisen to a post-war record of 148 vessels aggregating some 157,000 tons.

Mr Locke painted a rather gloomy picture for hull underwriting, with inadequate rates, disturbing casualty trends and escalating repair costs mitigating against any likelihood of a return to profitability. He condemned the number of breaches of the Joint Hull Understandings, either deliberately or inadvertantly through carelessness, and pointed out that if only one or two per cent of the market failed to honour the Understandings it could bring the agreement into jeopardy.

There was little comfort, either, for hull underwriters at this time in connection with laid-up tonnage. The amount of shipping in lay-up dropped from 1.35m tons in January 1964 to about 922,000 (out of a world total of 153m gross tons) in December of the same year, the latter figure representing some 125 vessels of which only fifteen were British. A dramatic improvement, this, over the figures for 1959 when some 9m tons out of a world total of 125m tons was laid up. But whilst this was a distinctly healthy sign for the shipping industry, it was beyond dispute that, when laid-up tonnage was at its peak in 1959, many Institute members enjoyed their best hull account for many years.

The size of large tankers and bulk carriers, meanwhile, continued to increase, reaching an average by the mid-60s of 57,000 deadweight tons compared with an average of 47,000 tons in 1960. But during the same year there were tankers on order at yards throughout the world exceeding 150,000 deadweight tons. These tonnage levels, which today seem singularly unremarkable, were regarded only twenty years ago as abnormally large, and the insured values of such vessels approached market capacity. The rating of these and other new vessels was the subject of some concern, with many underwriters claiming that the rates quoted by leaders erred on the side of generosity.

## A Problem Shared . . .

*Hull underwriters have seen some dramatic rises in ship sizes. Pictured is the "Esso Atlantic", at some 508,000 dwt one of the largest tankers in the world.*

One Institute Chairman, Mr P.G.L. Case, opened his statement for 1965 by describing the year as "an unhappy one in many ways." The India/Pakistan dispute, apart from its primary and inevitable results of loss of life and human suffering, found members of the Institute and other insurers facing numerous claims on vessels and cargoes caught up in the conflict. The War Risks Rating Committee was active during the same year as a result of the hostilities in Vietnam, India/Pakistan and Rhodesia.

The volume of laid-up shipping had fallen from 822,000 tons at the beginning of 1965 to just 572,000 by the end of December the same year, while the total volume of world tonnage had increased by over 7m gross tons between 1964 and 1965. Low levels of laid-up tonnage coupled with buoyant freight markets have traditionally boded ill for marine underwriters, and 1965 was no exception. The figures issued by the Liverpool Underwriters' Association showed that the number of total losses increased by over 30 per cent in 1965 compared with the average number from 1961 to 1964 and by the startling amount of 45 per cent (in terms of tonnage) over 1964. Partial losses had also increased considerably during the year.

Hurrican *Betsy* added considerably to the claims paid by many Institute members in their 1965 accounts and by the Autumn it was evident that members' fears for their 1964 hull accounts had become a grim reality. Delegates to the International Union of Marine Insurance conference held that year in Lucerne listened to a series of depressing reports which indicated that the time had come for action rather than talk unless the worst periods of the past such as those suffered in the 1920s were again to strike the marine market. It was a timely warning, and none the less sincere for its undoubted familiarity.

*An example of ship-building sophistication to meet changing trade requirements — the 27,400 cbm "Methane Princess", one of the earliest LPG carriers.*

ÆQUITAS ACTIONUM REGULA

# Chapter 8

# *Folkestone*

AFTER the devastation of much property in Central London by German air-raids during the Second World War, office accommodation was scarce and expensive and many businesses tried to move those parts of their operations which did not have to be located in the City out into provincial centres or country houses where costs would be lower and staff more readily available.

The Institute clearly needed more accommodation than it had prior to 1939, when the functions of the I.L.U. were mainly confined to general administration, the servicing of committees, research into general market problems and other like activities. The emergence of the Policy Department had resulted in a considerable growth in the activities of the Institute and in its staff levels, and this was to lead eventually to the opening of an office in Folkestone in 1965.

The following extracts from the Diaries of Philip Case, I.L.U. Chairman during 1964-65, perhaps best describe the reasons behind the decision to open the Folkestone office.

"On July 9, 1963, I had to take the Chair at the weekly meeting of the Institute for the first time as Leonard Locke was overseas. I made a note of some of the subjects we discussed. These included telling members for the first time of the committee's plans for setting up a country office, probably in Folkestone.

"For some years the management and committee of the Institute had realised that the time was fast approaching when additional office accommodation would have to be found for the non-administrative departments such as the Policy Signing Bureau and the Accounts Departments. The Institute was taking on more work for the benefit of member companies, centralisation and rationalisation being the order of the day. Office space within a reasonable distance of . . . Lime Street was almost impossible to obtain and that which was on offer could be obtained only at fantastically high rents. This was at a time when many businesses in Inner London were beginning to set up country offices where they could locate those departments whose physical presence in London was not essential. This had many advantages, not the least of which were cheaper rents and fewer travelling problems for staff, many of whom could be recruited locally. An investigation of the I.L.U. activities showed that the establishment of a country office should not adversely affect the efficiency of the Institute operations provided the new location was within 100 miles of London, as there would have to be a daily flow of paperwork between the offices independent of the postal service. After thorough investigations as to the suitability of various towns, it was eventually decided with the enthusiastic support of the local authority to set up a country office in Folkestone. A new purpose-built office block would be built for which finance would have to be arranged and developers appointed.

". . . Having decided on Folkestone we then set up a premises sub-committee on which I sat and at our first meeting on August 8 we agreed to approach Watling Street Properties for financing etc., but this did not get off the ground and it was with some trepidation that I proposed that an approach be made to my own company, the Norwich Union. The Norwich Union was already making its name as a property developer . . . and the society had built up an efficient Estates Department under the control of John Draper. My suggestion was well received both by my colleagues and by Norwich. On August 28, John Draper had his first meeting with the Premises Sub-Committee and the following day, at a full Institute Committee at which I took the chair for the first time, the decision was made to appoint the Norwich . . . For the rest of the year negotiations proceeded for the purchase of the land, the appointment of architects and the designing of the building.

"On January 7, 1964, we held an extraordinary general meeting of the I.L.U. to amend the Memorandum of Association to enable the Institute to own and to finance the offices we were to build in Folkestone. That same afternoon the Premises Sub-Committee met Mr Sutcliffe of the Norwich Union's Estates Department and Mr Hills of Messrs Howell and Brookes, the Norwich Union's architects, to study the plans they had drawn up for the new offices.

"On the morning of February 26, my wife accompanied me to the Grand Hotel Folkestone where the I.L.U. was giving a Press release at a reception followed by a buffet lunch attended by the Mayor, Miss Moody, Lord Folkestone and a large number of local dignitaries . . . I made a short speech of welcome to our guests after lunch to which Madam Mayor responded and later a number of us went to the site of our new building to select the brickwork from a number of samples built up into specimen walls. We adjourned to the Grand for an early tea. The local Folkestone newspaper responded nobly with a half-page feature article and two photographs . . . Describing the occasion, the paper said 'The year 1964 will be a boom one for Folkestone as far as office building is concerned. On May

Day a £150,000 office block is due to start rising on the site of the Pleasure Gardens Theatre to house over 150 staff of the Institute of London Underwriters.'

"A statement issued by the Institute said 'The new building has been designed as a country office and it is hoped that it will not create any feelings of dismay among those who are perhaps used to seeing green fields and trees. Our architects . . . have tried to incorporate a fair amount of landscape work which we hope will meet with the general approval of the local residents as well as satisfying the various other developers in the immediate vicinity, and of course provide happy working conditions for the staff. It is only a mild exaggeration to say that the new offices will be built around a computer room. The computer equipment, which is priced at about £133,000, will be rented from International Computers and Tabulators. Up to about 30 members of the existing staff of the Institute will be moving from London to Folkestone and it will be necessary to recruit at least 130 female staff locally. At a brief speech at Wednesday's reception, Mr P.G.L. Case . . . thanked the Mayor and Lord Folkestone for the way in which they and their organisations had received the proposals for the new offices. Half the site had been bought from Folkestone Estate, Lord Folkestone's company, and half from Folkestone Corporation. We look forward to the day in 1965 when we shall come to Folkestone for the purpose of opening our new building. In reply the Mayor said that Folkestone was delighted that the Institute should have decided to come here, that it was one of the finest things that had happened to the town for a long time, and that it was going to create a great deal of employment for the school leavers particularly.'

*The ILU's Folkestone premises — 'designed as a country office.'*

## A Problem Shared . . .

"On May 28, the Institute Committee agreed acceptance of the builder's tender for the Folkestone project and from then on I made frequent short trips to Folkestone to see how the work was proceeding. By November, the roof was on the computer wing and the Trinity Road wing was up to roof level. Progress was good and ahead of schedule.

"On July 7, 1965, a circular was sent by the Institute to all member companies informing them that the removal of the Policy Department from Lime Street to the new building in Folkestone would take place over the next weekend and that the office would be open at 9 a.m. on Monday, July 12.

"As Chairman of the Institute, I received the following telex message from Ridley in Folkestone on the morning of the 12th:— 'Operation Folkestone completed and although a few workmen are still about the staff were all working when I arrived at 9.45 a.m. Mr Hull and his team have worked a miracle over the weekend and indeed all through the operation. I have just addressed the staff in the canteen and welcomed them to their new offices.'

"On July 16, I was driven in an Institute car to Folkestone office where I was joined by all the Institute Committee and some guests for an official tour of inspection of our new building, after which I presided at a luncheon party in the Grand Hotel . . . Everyone satisfied and happy."

Lunch at the Grand Hotel and "Everyone satisfied and happy" might seem like lines from a Noel Coward play, but Philip Cases's words undoubtedly have the flavour of what was a time of expansion and achievement for the Institute. And the Folkestone office has certainly not stood still since its auspicious opening in 1965, nor been allowed to become an administrative backwater.

The Policy and Data Processing Departments at Folkestone operate a computer system which has been an essential tool for the provision of an ever-increasing range of services for members and through them the brokers with whom they transact business.

The adoption of Central Accounting was a natural progression in the growth of the modern centralised services offered by the ILU Policy Department. Some 500 company accounts are now handled with considerable benefit for over 100 members of the Institute and for approximately 350 firms of brokers.

In 1977, the Institute and Lloyd's Insurance Brokers' Association co-operated in the introduction of the Centralised Settlement Procedure, which was a natural extension of the Central Accounting System which had already been inaugurated. Mr. Bernard Curtis, by then Deputy Manager of the I.L.U., greatly assisted by Mr. A.W. Coles, London Accountant (Royal) was chiefly responsible for the organisation of this scheme which was so successful that it was said to be one of those rare instances of a new and complicated procedure being implemented without teething troubles.

*The innovative Sisu Container Mover, seen working in the port of Helsinki.*

The purpose of the Policy Department is to process risks written by company underwriters for the clients of brokers. This simple statement conceals a variety of effort. In brief, the process consists of the broker sending to the Policy Department the slip (a document showing the basic details of a risk). A coding and other information has already been entered. Subsequently these documents are individually checked for clerical and calculating errors and cross-checked with each other. The technical information is examined carefully and the bureau sheet then completed with the additional information required for data processing.

Information from the documents is then entered via Visual Display Units (VDUs) for processing through the computer system. This information is sufficient to prepare the closing advice sent to each member company participating in the risk and which includes such information as the policy number, line signed, the amount of premium due to the company and various technical details of the policy. A similar procedure is followed for additional premiums, return premiums and claims, and, taken altogether, the computer prints about 15,000 closing advices per day for despatch to companies plus about 1,200 advices for brokers. Including the various supporting journals, about 25,000 sheets are printed each day, resulting in a load of several hundredweight for the daily van-run to London.

The Central Accounting System produces a daily accounts journal for the companies, a monthly statement of deferred premiums, a monthly ledger and a settlement statement as between each company and each broker in the four accounting currencies.

The decision was made prior to centralised settlement to abandon the use of 162 convertible currencies which had to be held and converted using true rates of exchange. The rate of exchange is now shown before it is fed into the system and all currencies are expressed in Sterling, Canadian Dollars, U.S. Dollars, or, in the instance of converted currencies, in 'C£.'

The Central Accounting Scheme was itself a major advance on the practices of only two decades ago which required each broker to pay to each Company, or vice-versa, a cheque for each currency. The Centralised Settlement Procedure enables the payment to be made by one cheque from the broker or company to the Institute's Centralised Settlement Account, such payments being on a balance of account basis. These cheques are then paid into a special account at Lloyd's Bank and in the meantime the Bankers' Automated Clearing Services (BACS) will have received from the Institute's Data Processing Department a magnetic tape containing details of all payments due to brokers and companies. These amounts are then automatically paid from the special account to the various company and brokers' bank accounts concerned.

The Data Processing Department provides library facilities for policies, details of all policies received during the last 9 years being stored on magnetic disks. By this method, additional premiums, return premiums, claims, etc. on any of the policies issued during this period can be processed without the need for brokers to show all companies' lines, references, etc. on the bureau sheet, which in consequence saves all concerned much unnecessary work.

About 300 reinsurance treaty statements are received from brokers each day. Essential details of some 27,000 open treaties are held by the computer on magnetic disks and the information entered by VDUs from the statements is matched against this library in order to produce closing advices for companies. These advices are very comprehensive, showing information relating to the current closing plus up-to-date balances.

The equipment of the Institute has progressed from the 21-column punched-card system introduced in 1948 for internal statistics to two plugged board computers in the 1950's for a voluntary accounting system, then to an ICL 1500 computer installed in 1965 when the Policy Departments moved to Folkestone, through a subsequent mainframe computer and latterly to a mainframe and three minicomputers installed in 1979-80.

Each step has enabled the Institute to extend and improve its services to members, and the current system provides the means for the extensive services now rendered to the marine and aviation markets by the 190 staff of the Policy and Data Processing Departments in Folkestone and London.

Now almost twenty years old itself, the Folkestone office can reflect on the occasion of the Institute's centenary celebrations that it has established itself as an essential part of the I.L.U. operation.

AEQUITAS ACTIONUM REGULA

# Chapter 9

# The Centenary Approaches

JUST a few months after Mr Ridley had addressed the staff in the I.L.U. canteen at the new Folkestone office, there came the latest indication that hull insurers were still looking for that elusive profitability which had seemingly stayed at arm's length since the days of the coffee house transactions. The Joint Hull Committee on October 1, 1965, introduced new formulae for renewals which contained a flat rate addition of 5 per cent added to the minimum increases provided by the formulae. At the same time, automatic reductions for good figures were deleted and Canadian River and Inland Water Craft were brought within the scope of the Understandings.

Cargo underwriters, meanwhile, seemed to be more willing than at any time in the past to pull together for the good of the market. By 1965, a number of unofficial working parties consisting of company and Lloyd's cargo market leaders had begun to meet and issue reports and recommendations (which were made available to everyone in the market) concerning the underwriting of various commodities. "Such collaboration between Institute and Lloyd's members would have been unthinkable in the past", said one Institute Chairman, "but the two markets tend to co-operate in times of joint adversity."

Container traffic was by now increasing rapidly and attempts were being made to obtain cover on All Risks conditions, including full war and strikes risks at rates based not on the value of the cargo but on freight receipts and even on tonnage. Apart from the fact that this constituted a breach of the war risks rating agreement, the All Risks cover rates could well have proved to be totally inadequate when compared with premium calculated on the customary *ad valorem* basis.

Cargo underwriters were wondering if the introduction of containers for the carriage of cargo might prevent many in-transit losses, including those related to theft and pilferage. But the problem of ensuring that the containers remained sealed throughout the period of transit was even at this early stage causing great difficulties, and it was also quickly appreciated by the more discerning members of the underwriting community that any improvement in the claims situation as a result of the introduction of containerisation might rapidly be wiped out by insurers who granted over-compensatory rate reductions.

## A Problem Shared . . .

By 1967 it was obvious to the majority of hull underwriters that the rate increases which had been implemented would prove to be inadequate if the hull market was to recover from the disastrous slough of 1964 and 1965 and that underwriters had no option but to ask for heavier penalties, especially on 'singleton' vessels. Shipowners in some instances complained, but the truth was that for many years they had been enjoying a concealed subsidy from underwriters who, because of the highly competitive nature of the international market, had been writing risks with little consideration for factors such as the increased cost of repairs and poorer standards of crewing and maintenance.

Underwriters had also been over-optimistic in their assessment of premium requirements for the larger tonnage groups, in particular tankers and bulk carriers. Complaints were made during these years that insurers would quote inadequate premiums for new tonnage in the hope that if the business proved unsatisfactory the penalties provided by the Joint Hull Agreement would eventually put the matter right.

By the mid-1960s, another problem loomed large and ominous on the horizon of hull underwriting. This arose from the growing number of very large ships which were likely to replace a greater number of smaller vessels over which the risk had previously been spread. One example in these years was the loss of the *Torrey Canyon* which involved insurers in a loss in the region of $16m.

*The 1968-built "Q.E.II" — built when airlines had captured the Atlantic passenger market, to fulfill the twin functions of Atlantic service and worldwide cruising.*

During 1968, the Joint Hull Understandings were again amended. Category A, which had previously applied to single vessels, was amended to apply to one or two vessels, while the values of fleets falling under Categories B to E were increased by 15 per cent. A five completed years-basis for figures was also introduced. But although hull rates as a result continued an upward trend, with the Joint Hull Committee agreeing very few reductions even for good experience, the chairman of the Institute pointed out in his statement for 1968 that the general level of rating did no more than match that ruling in 1962, the last year in which many underwriters had recorded a profit. The liberal rate reductions of 1963, 1964 and 1965 were no more than contained by the rises achieved during the three following years.

In 1968, there was in fact a sharp increase in the commissioning of vessels of so-called "super" size. In 1962, the largest tanker afloat, the *Nissho Maru*, was of 130,000 deadweight tons, drawing 54 ft of water. By 1968 the tankers *Universe Ireland* and *Universe Kuwait* were of 276,000 d.w.t., drawing 79 ft. Their size and draught posed problems concerning arrangements for discharge and the need to navigate in certain areas with extreme precision. Underwriters who were concerned about the possible dangers that vessels of this size might offer knew full well that they faced during the next decade or two more risks arising from the commissioning of even more mammoth vessels.

Despite the growth of sophisticated navigational aids, serious casualties continued to occur with regularity. An example was the loss in 1968 of the New Zealand ferry *Wahine*, unfortunately with some loss of life, in quite abnormal weather conditions. And December 1969 brought the loss of the tanker *Marpessa*, at 104,000 g.r.t. the largest vessel to have been lost at that time.

It can be seen that increases in hull rates were essential if underwriters were to keep incurring such heavy losses, but perhaps of equal significance at this time was the request made by the Joint Hull Committee to the Technical and Clauses Committee to revise the Institute Time Clauses and all ancillary clauses by introducing a "deductible each accident" basis together with an alteration to the Inchmaree Clause, thus providing a degree of self-insurance for negligence claims. It had been estimated that by 1969 rates should have been about 25 per cent above those ruling in 1962. The Joint Hull Formula was at this time designed to cope with a steady rate of inflation of up to 5 per cent each year. When towards the end of the decade the Government's Prices and Incomes Policy was relaxed, members of the I.L.U. were faced with the realisation that the 1970s could start by opening the floodgates of inflation when renewal at expiring rates would mean not only a virtual 5 per cent reduction but one amounting to 10 or even 15 per cent.

## A Problem Shared . . .

The month of December 1969 saw three explosions in large tankers which resulted in the sinking of the *Marpessa* and in very serious damage to the *Mactra* and the *Kong Haakon VII*. At the time of these casualties, some 60 tankers of comparable size (over 100,000 gross tons) were in service while another 165 were on order.

The new hull clauses introduced on October 1, 1969 were amended in some respects the following year due to criticisms made by average adjusters, brokers and others, but the main amendment relating to the use of deductibles in place of franchises had by this time become accepted market practice in both London and overseas. Apart from its more immediate object of eliminating small claims and reducing the size of others, this had the effect of making owners far more attentive in matters of selection, supervision and training of personnel, in which during the 1960s there was thought to have been some failure by shipowners in attaining an adequate standard.

The three casualties of December 1969 gave an impetus to revise rates on large tankers renewed during 1970, and the support given to the recommended guidelines for large bulk carriers and tankers indicated that insurers were thinking more realistically of the risks involved and the need for higher premiums.

The effect of inflation remained one of the greatest problems facing underwriters at the end of the 1960s, a factor which doubtless played a big part in the decision to revise levels of rating and terms of coverage for building risks in July 1970. It was a sobering thought perhaps that any progress which had been made over the years towards obtaining a reasonable underwriting profit by the application of realistic rates and reformed conditions had been severely reduced by the effects of inflation on repair costs. At the end of the 1960s, some underwriters expressed the hope that inflation, then running at between 12 and 13 per cent, would drop considerably during the 1970s. Perhaps it was as well that they could not see too far into the future.

For many years, successive I.L.U. Chairmen could find little good to say in their statements about the cargo side of the Institute market. It must therefore have come as something of a surprise when in January 1970 the Institute Chairman, Mr G. Donald Taylor, said that he turned "with a sigh of relief, even if only relatively, to cargo." The 'Consult the Lead' Agreement was working quite well, while various working parties had produced reports dealing with a large number of different commodities. While cargo insurance was not especially vulnerable to inflation, it was affected by the high level of major casualties which occurred during these years and of course by the social problems of the time which led, among other things, to a further increase in the incidence of theft and pilferage losses.

The use of containers tended to reduce the number of small pilferage and damage claims, but when losses did occur they were found to be heavier than in non-containerised shipments. One reason for this was that the entry of seawater or fresh water into the container, or the breaking-up of stowed goods, tended to go unnoticed until the container was opened at the final point of destination. Another problem involved the hi-jacking of whole container loads of such 'desirable' goods as whisky and cigarettes, which was not helped by the lack of security in many instances when containers were parked within the confines of ports or delayed whilst in transit and their whereabouts and contents quickly became known to the highly efficient gangs of thieves operating in and around the ports and warehouses and on the motorways.

*A mysterious casualty — the 223,963 dwt ore/oil carrier "Berge Vanga" vanished without trace, one of an enormous number of large and expensive hull casualties to hit the market in the late 1970s/early 1980s.*

On another front, it should be noted that, during the early 1970s, following the expansion of the aviation market, two companies (British Aviation Insurance Company and Aviation and General Insurance Company) became associate members and, later, full members of the I.L.U. Premium income from the aviation market was by now assuming increasing importance. Today, it accounts for about 30 per cent of all business processed through the Institute.

There had always been close co-operation between the I.L.U. and the Liverpool Underwriters' Association on many matters of mutual interest such as clauses, the Joint Hull Understandings and the invaluable Liverpool casualty statistics. But on July 1, 1970, the connection between the two organisations became closer still when the Liverpool Underwriters' Association became an affiliate member of the I.L.U. while still retaining its separate identity. The members of the two bodies considered that this closer relationship would enable the British company marine

# A Problem Shared . . .

insurance market to be more appropriately represented in negotiations in the international field, and the new decade was certainly one in which international negotiations looked like being of even more importance than in the previous one.

There was undoubtedly much of a non-domestic nature to occupy the Institute's time in the early 1970s. In 1970 alone there were the troubles in Northern Ireland, the aftermath of the civil war in Nigeria, continued inflation, another dollar crisis, the continuation of hostilities in Vietnam, the decision to nationalise general insurance business in India, and the war between India and Pakistan.

In 1971, several meetings and discussions took place between Institute members and Lloyd's underwriters and brokers in connection with a proposed Terms of Credit Scheme. Maximum periods of credit for all classes of business were agreed during this year, although no final decision was reached concerning the mechanics or the administration of this scheme.

*Today, aviation business accounts for something like 30 per cent of all transactions processed through the ILU.*

112

Although hull underwriters in these early years of the 1970s might well have been hoping for some improvement in the results of their business, it was generally thought that they would do well to achieve anything more than a break-even position. The long-awaited return to profitability in hull underwriting was still a long time coming.

But there was certainly no shortage of willing takers. At the end of 1972, the Institute approved revised Articles of Association which provided, amongst other things, for the admittance of associate members, mainly from overseas companies. Within a year, 232 new applications for associate membership had been accepted, this influx of fresh capacity coinciding with the U.K.'s entry into the European Economic Community and the prospects that it brought of closer co-operation between the new partners.

It was perhaps mere coincidence that during this same year the marine underwriting market of one of the E.E.C. countries experienced what Institute Chairman Mr W.J. Claydon described in January 1974 as "the most difficult year of its existence." The previous year had in fact seen the reconstruction of the Joint Hull Committee, which at the time was facing what Mr Claydon called "reckless and irresponsible attacks both internationally and from within the London market itself." Mr Claydon felt that the forebearance and tenacity of the Joint Hull Committee members offered "a glimmer of hope for the future of the hull market."

The mid-1970s saw the marine insurance market once again entering one of its regular troughs, with hull insurance chronically unprofitable. This was a period of intense competition for hull business, with a surfeit of worldwide capacity for all risks and rates threatening to hit rock-bottom. It is a scenario which has occurred with irritating regularity throughout the history of the marine insurance market, and one with which today's underwriters will be only too familiar. But what the underwriters of the mid-1970s could not know was that the situation was going to get worse before it got better.

But even then the prospects for a quick recovery did not look too bright. In 1974, the Salvage Association estimated that the effect of inflation on repair costs was in excess of 20 per cent in every major repairing country. During the same year, a leading company hull underwriter said that, since 1972, London underwriters had been forced to yield to such intensive competition that, by mid-1974, hull rates were some 40 per cent below the 1971-72 level.

While underwriters were coping with the problems of inadequate premiums, they were concerned also at this time with getting into their books that premium which was due them. Despite the limited success of the Terms of Credit Scheme, underwriters were unhappy with the manner in which some brokers delayed premium payments, in some cases quite unreasonably.

## A Problem Shared . . .

During the latter part of the 1970s, international competition became even more intense both in the hull and the cargo market, accompanied this time by a marked decline in worldwide trade which saw many ships moving into lay-up berths. But there was no reduction in the level of claims. Indeed, 1977 was a peak year for total losses in terms of both numbers of vessels and of tonnage.

In the cargo market, the art of containerisation continued to develop apace, although some of those claims which the 'box trade' was supposed to eliminate still occurred with uncomfortable regularity. Claims from

*Containerisation continued to develop apace —*

breaking and denting, freshwater damage and theft and pilferage were apparently no great advertisement for the supposed protection afforded by the container, although such damage was due in many cases no doubt to the fact that the packing *inside* the container had been reduced to an absolute bare minimum.

*— but so did the casualties.*

*(Laurence Dunn)*

114

It was hardly surprising, then, that preparations got under way in these years for the formulation of a Convention on the Carriage of Goods by Sea which was intended to place a greater responsibility and liability on the shipowner for loss of or damage to cargo. Institute underwriters, together with their colleagues at Lloyd's, played an important role in the drafting of this convention.

The 1970s drew to a close with the international marine insurance market seemingly affected by just about every malady but rising damp:—overcapacity, severe competition between international brokers and underwriters, marine fraud and a steadily worsening casualty situation, to name only the most persistent of these. The 1979 year of account was talked of as the most appalling on record and it is perhaps worthy of closer examination here.

The Liverpool Underwriters' figures showed that 1979 had produced the worst casualty situation ever encountered in peacetime. There were 279 total losses aggregating 2.265m tons gross. The tonnage lost exceeded by 64 per cent the 1978 figure which was then itself the highest on record.

One Institute underwriter went on record in 1979 as saying that, if the amended Joint Hull Understandings of that year were not accepted, the Joint Hull Committee would be disbanded and put aside. At the International Union of Marine Insurance Conference in Edinburgh later that year, the same underwriter said that insurers in London had supported the Understandings wholeheartedly and that "if our business is to be governed by the criterion of investment income, we stand a very great danger that our business will be destroyed — and, more important, there cannot be a lasting benefit to our clients." He added that, unless there was a dramatic improvement in the forthcoming hull renewal season, there would be little point in anybody coming to the next IUMI Conference "because we will only be wasting our time."

The fact that underwriters *did* gather in 1980 for the IUMI Conference in Seattle perhaps says less about the fact that underwriters heeded this warning than it does about the extraordinary and sometimes misguided determination of some sections of the international marine insurance market to weather almost any problem without actually taking steps to put it right at source. It is true that there was a modest reduction in the amount of tonnage lost in 1980, but the I.L.U. report nevertheless referred to that year as "one of the most difficult and tantalising on record". Inevitably, hull rates were exposed once again as being hopelessly inadequate and it was not without significance that the Chairman of the Joint Hull Committee told delegates to the 1980 IUMI Conference that many underwriters felt they had "a divine right to lose money" and were now, in fact, not underwriting but under-*rating*.

## A Problem Shared . . .

Predictably, the under-rating carried over into 1981, when the Chairman of the IUMI Ocean Hull Committee said "We may as well start thinking of early retirement if, as has been suggested, competition for hull business is now so strong that nothing can be done about it."

At the same time it was reported that there had been a worldwide decline in cargo underwriting standards, with rates cut to the bone and terms of coverage widened considerably. There was general concern for the future of cargo insurance which was lent further emphasis the following year when a number of cargo underwriters pointed to the deterioration of standards in their national markets. The message from hull underwriters at the same time was also sickeningly familiar, with the IUMI Ocean Hull Committee Chairman in 1982 remarking that insurers were "slowly bleeding to death."

One of the big problems of the late-1970s and the early-1980s was the availability of cheap reinsurance protection, on the strength of which so

*The 125,000 cbm LNG carrier "Libra" — what would the hull underwriter of 1884 make of such a creature?*

many direct insurers overwrote and underrated both hull and cargo risks. By the end of 1983, there were signs that some sanity was at last beginning to return to the hull insurance market following two successive years of tough renewals for reinsurance business. On both proportional treaty and

*A fine example of the sophistication of passenger shipping in the 1980s — "Norway" (formerly the trans-Atlantic liner "France") converted at a cost of some £45m.*

excess loss business, underwriters called for rate increases and restrictions in cover, as well as cutting back on commission levels and the like. These developments were welcomed by many leading hull underwriters as the most encouraging signs for years. Furthermore, they were accompanied by an improvement, albeit a marginal and in some respects disappointing one, in the casualty situation.

Sadly, cargo business appeared to be headed in the opposite direction. At the beginning of 1983, it was announced that a joint working party commissioned by the Institute and Lloyd's Underwriters' Association had produced a hard-hitting report on cargo insurance. Amongst other things, this identified deposit premiums, the presentation of renewal figures, master covers and slip discounts as areas of 'major concern'. At the 99th Annual General Meeting of the I.L.U. in 1983, Chairman Mr Tony Nunn said that many of the cargo market's problems were self-inflicted and that

## A Problem Shared . . .

". . . we cannot solely blame 'other markets' for the totally inadequate basic premium charged. Basic principles have been forgotten. It is no good charging the F.P.A. rate of 1972 as the All Risks rate of 1982."

Further confirmation of the depressed state of the cargo market came at the International Union of Marine Insurance Conference in 1983 when a report in similar vein written by a leading cargo underwriter in the

*Hardly recognisable as a ship at all — "Super Servant 3" carrying three offshore barges, and taking marine underwriting techniques into entirely new areas.*

company market was presented to delegates in Florence. For the first time in a number of years, it was now cargo insurance which was causing the greatest concern — and, not for the first time, underwriters of marine insurance were discovering the truth of that old adage about losing on the roundabouts what they might have gained on the swings.

per Servant 4', a self-propelled, semi-submersible, heavy lift
rier. The underwater shadow is the vessel's submerged deck.

*Collision victim — the Townsend Thoresen ferry "European Gateway" represents a forlorn spectacle for her owners, and doubtless for her underwriters too.*

*Inside the "European Gateway".*

# Chapter 10

# Joint Committees

BEFORE finally coming up to date, it is necessary to take a brief look at the valuable work undertaken by the Institute in connection with the various representative committees which have become synonomous with the marine insurance market.

Apart from providing the secretariat for its own committees, the Institute has traditionally been responsible for the running of the many joint market committees and subcommittees which include representatives of Lloyd's Underwriters' Association. These joint committees are extremely valuable in that they provide means for the whole market to formulate policies or take common action where it is felt desirable.

The Joint Hull Committee is the oldest of these committees, dating back to 1910. It meets to discuss all matters connected with hull insurance, including developments in the shipping industry. An example of its work is the recently introduced inert gas systems warranty which imposes an obligation on owners who have installed such a system to ensure that it is fully approved by the classification society with which the vessel is classed and operated in accordance with laid-down instructions. A small section of the ILU London staff forms the Joint Hull Returns Bureau which examines all applications from shipowners for lay-up returns and has full powers to approve or reject them on behalf of underwriters. Approval of a return will depend primarily on the location of the vessel throughout the period of lay-up, but the amount of return is determined by the policy conditions and the port-risk retentions applicable to those conditions. An appeal against a decision by the bureau can be made to the Joint Hull Committee and will be dealt with by a special returns subcommittee.

The Joint Constructions Risks Committee (1933, though as a companies-only committee dating back to 1909) functions similarly to the Joint Hull Committee but in the field of shipbuilding risks.

The Joint Cargo Committee (1942) deals, as its name implies, with the other main field of marine insurance. This includes cargo by air as well as by sea.

The War Risks Rating Committee (1935) keeps under close surveillance situations in various parts of the world which might affect the insurance of war risks for cargoes, and forms the only 'tariff' section of the London

## A Problem Shared . . .

marine and aviation markets. When any change in the rating for an area is decided upon it is notified immediately to all other marine insurance associations across the world.

The Technical and Clauses Committee (1925), members of which are drawn from company and Lloyd's underwriters and claims adjusters, acts on mandates from the main committees to revise existing clauses or introduce new ones. With the large number of standard clauses in use it faces a heavy task, particularly having recently completed one major revision and with another in its later stages. The Institute clauses it produces are the basis of cover granted by the market, with additional wordings produced to tailor a particular insurance direct to the needs of the assured. Institute clauses have a wide currency internationally and are used or adapted by many other markets.

*A most unusual loss — the Liberian-owned tanker "Hercules" going down off the Brazilian coast, an indirect casualty of the Falklands war. It was decided to sink the vessel after efforts to remove an unexploded bomb had proved too risky.*

The Joint Liability Committee (established in 1974 as the Joint Carriers' Liability Committee) is the most recently formed market committee. It co-ordinates the work of market representatives on a number of bodies, such as the International Chamber of Commerce, dealing with questions of maritime liabilities and documentation. It took an active part in the consultations leading up to the adoption in 1978 of the Hamburg Rules (regulating the contractual relationship between sea carriers and cargo owners), and most recently in May 1980 the adoption by UNCTAD of the multi-modal convention regulating the contractual relationship in transport involving more than one mode of carriage, something that has grown very quickly in recent years with the spread of container transport. In each case the Joint Liability Committee sent advisers to assist the UK delegation at the diplomatic conference which adopted those conventions.

*Offshore oil exploration has opened up a new area of activity for today's marine underwriter.*

The committee also participates in the work of the British Maritime Law Association, the body which co-ordinates the views of the various sectors of the shipping industry and includes both the London marine market, underwriting hull and cargo business, and the Protection & Indemnity Clubs underwriting shipowners' liabilities in mutual associations.

The Institute also takes a leading role in the activities of the International Union of Marine Insurance (IUMI). Many underwriters of Institute member companies serve on IUMI committees and each year a delegation is sent to IUMI conferences. The last conference held in the UK was at Edinburgh in 1979 and was organised by the Institute of London Underwriters as joint hosts with Lloyd's Underwriters' Association.

*The 271,540 dwt "Castillo de Bellver" meets an untimely end off Cape Town. With a combined hull and cargo value of £45m, this was the largest ship lost in the 1983 underwriting year.*

# Chapter 11

# *Full Circle*

AND so to 1984. No doubt those underwriters who slaked their thirsts in the Jerusalem Coffee House before cutting along to those early Institute meetings in the Royal Exchange Buildings would raise their eyebrows at some of the events in the market today. Much has happened during the 100 years of the Institute's existence, and the market has recently witnessed what is arguably the most fundamental revision of marine insurance terms and conditions ever undertaken. In 1982 and 1983, new Institute Cargo Clauses and Institute Time Clauses — Hulls were introduced by London underwriters following several years of hard work, to which added stimulus was given by the report of the United Nations Conference on Trade and Development on the Legal and Documentary Aspects of Marine Insurance, which contained a critical assessment of marine insurance practice and methods. The much-abused S.G. form of policy has now at last been superseded, and the pessimists sit back and wait for a whole new set of legal precedents to be established while the optimists look ahead to the day when all marine interests will understand their insurance policies. The policy itself now contains a minimum of detail to be amplified by the attachment of the relevant new clauses.

This is a fundamental change indeed, and there was a hint of further innovative developments on a more general level when Tony Nunn addressed the Institute's annual meeting in 1983. Speaking in a suitably Orwellian vein, Mr Nunn announced that a sub-committee had recently been formed to review 'The Future of the I.L.U.' and that he was greatly encouraged by the enthusiasm and ideas that had already come from the new unit, which would apparently be making 'far-reaching recommendations.' Mr Nunn provided a clue to the direction which the Institute might be taking in the years ahead, referring to such matters as office economies, the mechanics of maintaining an underwriting office, and the possibility in the not-too-distant future of underwriters and brokers conducting their business by means of desk-top television sets and the like.

Certainly the Institute of London Underwriters has come an awfully long way in its 100 years of existence. Like any worthwhile institution, it has not only moved with and adapted to changes in its own industry and the industries which it serves, it has when necessary precipitated changes

**A Problem Shared . . .**

of its own. Time and again during the past century it has shown the value of harnessing the underwriting talents of its members for the good of the market. It is, and has been for many, many years, an indispensable part of both the London and the international marine insurance underwriting scene.

Having just looked back on 100 years of the I.L.U.'s existence, it is a sobering thought that, in many respects, the underwriters of today have been unable to solve the problems which dogged their predecessors. Consider for a moment the following statements:—

"No-one can be gloomy all the time and the occasional straw flutters by in the wind to cheer us up, but one cannot avoid the reality that the underlying basis of general marine underwriting remains unsound."

"There is a decided tendency to stiffen rates, and if a general move could

*D. Town, Chairman of the I.L.U. for centenary year.*

126

be made and adhered to, better rates could be obtained. The London companies were not over-fortunate last year, nor were Lloyd's underwriters. The reason is clear. The premiums have been too low.''

Although the message is much the same, the two remarks are separated by 100 years, one having been made in 1883 and the other in 1983. The trick is deciding which is which.

While so much has changed in the last 100 years, and while today's underwriter has bigger and more expensive vessels and cargoes to insure and such new developments as containerisation, and offshore and nuclear risks to consider, the marine insurance industry's greatest problem — how to write its risks at realistic rates on prudent conditions — remains unsolved. The wheel has turned a full circle but, in turning, has left much of fundamental importance largely untouched.

*D.D. Lowen, Deputy Chairman*

*B.D. Curtis, General Manager & Secretary.*

# *Appendices*

## THE "1888 CLAUSES"

### AS RECOMMENDED BY THE
### INSTITUTE OF LONDON UNDERWRITERS

### FOR ADOPTION IN THE YEAR'S POLICIES ON HULLS

And it is further agreed that if the ship hereby insured shall come into collision with any other ship or vessel, and the assured shall in consequence thereof become liable to pay, and shall pay by way of damages to any other person or persons any sum or sums not exceeding in respect of any one such collision the value of the ship hereby insured, this Company will pay the assured such proportion of three-fourths of such sum or sums so paid as its subscription hereto bears to the value of the ship hereby insured, and in cases in which the liability of the ship has been contested with the consent in writing of this Company, the Company will also pay a like proportion of three-fourths of the costs which the assured shall thereby incur or be compelled to pay.

Provided always that this Clause shall in no case extend to any sum which the assured may become liable to pay, or shall pay for removal of obstructions under statutory powers, for injury to harbours, wharves, piers, stages, and similar structures, consequent on such collision, or in respect of the cargo or engagements of the insured vessel, or for loss of life or personal injury.

The warranty and conditions as to average under 3 per cent to be applicable to each voyage as if separately insured, and not to the whole time insured.

In port and at sea, in docks and graving docks, and on ways, gridirons and pontoons, at all times, in all places, and on all occasions, services and trades whatsoever and wheresoever, under steam or sail, with leave to sail with or without pilots, to tow and assist vessels or craft in all situations, and to be towed and to go on trial trips.

Average payable on each valuation separately or on the whole, without deduction of thirds, new for old, whether the average be particular or general.

General Average and Salvage Charges payable according to foreign statement, or per York-Antwerp rules if in accordances with the contract of affreightment.

## A Problem Shared . . .

In the event of deviation from the terms and conditions of this Policy, it is hereby agreed to hold the assured covered, premium to be arranged, provided due notice be given by the assured on receipt of advices of such deviation.

Should the above vessel be at sea on the expiration of this policy, it is agreed to hold her covered until arrival at port of destination, or until lost, at a pro rata monthly premium, if so desired by the owners.

To return {
    per cent for each uncommenced month if this Policy be cancelled.
    as follows for each consecutive 30 days the vessel may be laid up in port unemployed, viz:—
        per cent if in the United Kingdom not under Average.
        per cent under Average, or if abroad not under Average.
} and arrival

This insurance also specially to cover loss of, or damage to hull or machinery through the negligence of Master Mariners, Engineers, or Pilots, or through explosions, bursting of boilers, breakage of shafts, or through any latent defect in the machinery or hull, provided such loss or damage has not resulted from want of due diligence by the owners of the vessel, or any of them, or by the manager.

Donkey boilers, winches, cranes, windlasses, steering gear, and electric light apparatus shall be deemed to be part of the hull, and not part of the machinery.

No claim shall be allowed in consequence of the vessel having been stranded, except for such expenses as may be incurred for the purposes of sighting the vessel's bottom, and the execution of such work as the surveyor may require to have the vessel surveyed and repaired, and that no damages occurring on any one voyage shall be allowed unless they by themselves or together with any particular average consequent on stranding on the same voyage amount to 3 per cent.

No claim shall be allowed in respect of scraping and painting the vessel's bottom, whether the ship be stranded or not.

For the purposes of average the word "voyage" shall be defined to be that period within which two cargoes are delivered, excepting where an outward or homeward passage is made in ballast, when the period shall close on the delivery of one cargo. If discharging at a port on the Continent, it shall include the passage in ballast to a port in the United Kingdom, but if discharging in the United Kingdom, the voyage shall terminate at the port of delivery of cargo.

In the event of accident whereby loss or damage may result in a claim under this Policy, notice must be given in writing to this Company where practicable prior to survey, so that they may appoint their own Surveyor if desired.

Grounding in the Suez Canal, or in the Rivers Parana, Danube, Demerara, or Bilbao, or on Yenikale or Bilbao Bars, shall not be deemed to be a stranding.

The insured value to be mutually admitted and taken to be the sound value of the ship for all purposes of loss under this Policy.

## THE "1889 CLAUSES"

### AS RECOMMENDED BY THE
### INSTITUTE OF LONDON UNDERWRITERS
### FOR ADOPTION IN THE YEAR'S POLICIES ON HULLS

And it is further agreed that if the ship hereby insured shall come into collision with any other ship or vessel, and the Assured shall in consequence thereof become liable to pay and shall pay by way of damages to any other person or persons any sum or sums not exceeding in respect of any one such collision the value of the ship hereby insured, this Company will pay the Assured such proportion of three-fourths of such sum or sums so paid as its subscription hereto bears to the value of the ship hereby insured, and in cases in which the liability of the ship has been contested with the consent in writing of this Company, the Company will also pay a like proportion of three-fourths of the costs which the Assured shall thereby incur or be compelled to pay.

Provided always that this Clause shall in no case extend to any sum which the Assured may become liable to pay, or shall pay for removal of obstructions under statutory powers, for injury to harbours, wharves, piers, stages and similar structures, consequent on such collision, or in respect of the cargo or engagements of the insured vessel, or for loss of life or personal injury.

In port and at sea, in docks and graving docks, and on ways, gridirons and pontoons, at all times, in all places, and on all occasions, services and trades whatsoever and wheresoever, under steam or sail, with leave to sail with or without pilots, to tow and assist vessels or craft in all situations, and to be towed and to go on trial trips.

Should the above vessel be at sea on the expiration of this Policy, it is agreed to hold her covered until arrival at port of destination, or until lost, whichever may first occur, at a pro rata monthly premium, provided due notice be given before the expiration of the Policy, and damage during such extension shall be treated as if it had occurred during the final voyage under this Policy for the purposes of the warranty as to average.

Held covered in case of deviation, change of voyage, or breach of warranty as to trade or locality, provided notice be given and any additional premium required be paid immediately after receipt of advices.

This insurance also specially to cover loss of, or damage to hull or machinery through the negligence of master, mariners, engineers, or pilots, or through explosions, bursting of boilers, breakage of shafts, or through any latent defect in the machinery or hull, provided such loss or damage has not resulted from want of due diligence by the owners of the ship, or any of them, or by the manager.

General Average and Salvage Charges payable according to Foreign statement, or per York-Antwerp rules if in accordance with the contract of affreightment.

Average payable on each valuation separately or on the whole, without deduction of thirds, new for old, whether the Average be particular or general.

Donkey boilers, winches, cranes, windlasses, steering gear and electric light apparatus shall be deemed to be part of the hull, and not part of the machinery.

Warranted free from particular average under 3 per cent, but nevertheless when the vessel shall have been stranded, sunk, or on fire, Underwriters to pay the damage occasioned thereby. No claim shall be allowed in respect of scraping or painting the vessel's bottom, whether she be stranded or not; but the expense of sighting the bottom after stranding shall be paid, if reasonably incurred, even if no damage be found.

Grounding in the Suez Canal, or in the Rivers Parana, Danube, Demerara, or Bilbao, or on Yenikale or Bilbao Bars, shall not be deemed to be a stranding.

The warranty and conditions as to average under 3 per cent, to be applicable to each voyage as if separately insured, and not to the whole time insured, and a voyage shall commence at one of the following periods, to be selected by the Assured (at any time whether before or after any damage shall have occurred), viz., at the inception of the Policy, or any time during the currency thereof, at which the vessel, being empty or in ballast or engaged in completing the discharge of the previous cargo, begins to load cargo, or sails in ballast under Charter to a loading port; and unless the Policy shall previously expire, any such voyage shall be deemed to continue during the ensuing period within which two cargoes are in course of carriage or discharge, and until the vessel begins to load a third cargo or sails in ballast under Charter for a loading port; but the commencement of any voyage shall not be so fixed as to overlap the termination of the previous voyage in respect of which there is a claim.

In no case shall Underwriters be liable for unrepaired damage in addition to a subsequent total loss sustained during the original or extended term covered by this Policy.

The insured value to be mutually admitted and taken to be the sound value of the ship for all purposes of loss under this Policy.

In the event of accident whereby loss or damage may result in a claim under this Policy, notice shall be given in writing to the Underwriters, where practicable prior to survey, so that they may appoint their own Surveyor if desired.

Warranted free from capture, seizure, and detention, the consequences thereof, or of any attempt thereat, unless arising from piracy or barratry, and from all consequences of hostilities or warlike operations, whether before or after declaration of war.

To return { per cent for each uncommenced month if this Policy be cancelled. as follows for each consecutive 30 days the vessel may be laid up in port unemployed, viz:— per cent if in the United Kingdom not under Average. per cent under Average, or if abroad not under Average. } and arrival

## THE "1890 CLAUSES"

The 1890 Clauses are the same as the 1888 Clauses, above, with the following exceptions, viz:—

(1) The Running Down Clause. After the words . . . . . . "compelled to pay" add:— "but when both vessels are to blame, then unless the liability of the owners of one or both of such vessels becomes limited by law, claims under this clause shall be settled on the principle of cross-liabilities as if the owners of each vessel had been compelled to pay to the owners of the other of such vessels such one-half or other proportion of the latter's damages as may have been properly allowed in ascertaining the balance or sum payable by or to the Assured in consequence of such collision."

(2) Donkey Boilers and Winches. Add:— "Refrigerating machinery and insulation not covered unless expressly included in this Policy."

(3) The Valuation Clause. Amended as follows:— "The Insured value to be mutually admitted and taken to be the sound value of the ship in all questions of Constructive Total Loss under this Policy."

**A Problem Shared . . .**

## THE INSTITUTE OF LONDON UNDERWRITERS
# Members
at 31 March, 1984

Albion Insurance Co., Ltd.
Alliance Assurance Co., Ltd.
Allianz International Insurance Co., Ltd.
Andrew Weir Insurance Co., Ltd.
Assicurazioni Generali S.p.A.
Assurances Generales de France I.A.R.T.
Assurances du Groupe de Paris R.D.
Atlantic Mutual Insurance Co.
Atlas Assurance Co., Ltd.
Aviation & General Insurance Co., Ltd.
Baloise Insurance Co., Ltd.
Baltica-Skandinavia Insurance Co. (U.K.) Ltd.
Bishopsgate Insurance PLC
British Aviation Insurance Co., Ltd.
British & Foreign Marine Insurance Co., Ltd.
British Law Insurance Co., Ltd.
Caledonian Insurance Co.
Century Insurance Co., Ltd.
Colonia Insurance Co. (U.K.) Ltd.
Commercial Union Assurance Co. plc.
Compagnie d'Assurances Maritimes Aeriennes et
  Terrestres
la Concorde Compagnie d'Assurances Contre les
  Risques de Toute Nature
Continental Insurance Co. (U.K.) Ltd.
Cornhill Insurance PLC
Dai-Tokyo Insurance Co. (U.K.) Ltd.
Dowa Insurance Company (U.K.) Ltd.
Eagle Star Insurance Co., Ltd.
English & American Insurance Co., Ltd.
English & Scottish Maritime & General Insurance
  Co. Ltd.
Excess Insurance Co., Ltd.
Federal Insurance Co.
Folksam International Insurance Co. (U.K.) Ltd.
Forsikringsaktieselskabet Hafnia: trading as
  Danish Marine Insurance Company (Hafnia)
GAN Incendie Accidents
General Accident Fire & Life Assurance Corp.,
  p.l.c.
General Accident Reinsurance Co., Ltd.
Guardian Royal Exchange Assurance plc
Hansa Marine Insurance Co. (U.K.) Ltd.
Hibernian Insurance Co., Ltd.
Home Insurance Co.
Indemnity Marine Assurance Co., Ltd.
Insurance Company of North America (U.K.) Ltd.
Insurance Corporation of Ireland, Ltd.
Leadenhall Insurance PLC
Legal & General Assurance Society Ltd.
Liberty Mutual Insurance Company
  (Massachusetts) Ltd.
Liverpool Marine & General Insurance Co., Ltd.
Lombard Elizabethan Insurance plc
London & Aachen Munich Marine
  Insurance Co., Ltd.
London Assurance
London & Hull Maritime Insurance Co. Ltd.

London & Overseas Insurance Co., P.L.C.
London Guarantee & Reinsurance Co., Ltd.
Malvern Insurance Co., Ltd.
Marine Insurance Co., Ltd.
Maritime Insurance Co., Ltd.
Mercantile and General Reinsurance Co. plc
Minster Insurance Co., Ltd.
National Employers' Mutual General Insurance
  Association Ltd.
National Insurance Co. of New Zealand, Ltd.
Navigators & General Insurance Co., Ltd.
New Hampshire Insurance Co.
New India Assurance Co., Ltd.
New Zealand South British Insurance PLC
Nippon Fire & Marine Insurance Co. (U.K.) Ltd.
Northern Assurance Co., Ltd.
Northern Maritime Insurance Co., Ltd.
Norwich Union Fire Insurance Society Ltd.
Ocean Marine Insurance Co., Ltd.
Orion Insurance Co., P.L.C.
Pearl Assurance Public Limited Company
Phoenix Assurance Public Limited Company
Planet Assurance Co., Ltd.
Pohjola Insurance Co. (U.K.) Ltd.
Polaris Assuranse A/S
Preservatrice Fonciere T.I.A.R.D.
La Providence I.A.R.D.
Prudential Assurance Co., Ltd.
la Reunion Francaise Soc. Anon. d'Assurances et
  des Reassurances
River Thames Insurance Co., Ltd.
Road Transport & General Insurance Co., Ltd.
Royal Exchange Assurance
Royal Insurance (U.K.) Ltd.
Sea Insurance Co. Ltd.
Sirius Insurance Co. (U.K.) Ltd.
Skandia U.K. Insurance p.l.c.
Sovereign Marine & General Insurance Co., Ltd.
Sphere Drake Insurance plc
Storebrand Insurance Co. (U.K.) Ltd.
Sumitomo Marine & Fire Insurance Co. (Europe) Ltd.
Sun Insurance Office, Ltd.
Swiss Reinsurance Co. (U.K.) Ltd.
Switzerland General Insurance Co. (London) Ltd.
Taisho Marine & Fire Insurance Co. (U.K.) Ltd.
Theadneedle Insurance Co., Ltd.
Tokio Marine & Fire Insurance Co. (U.K.) Ltd.
Turegum Insurance Co.
Ulster Marine Insurance Co., Ltd.
L'Union des Assurances de Paris I.A.R.D.
Union Marine & General Insurance Co., Ltd.
Vesta (U.K.) Insurance Co., Ltd.
Victory Reinsurance Co., Ltd.
Westminster Fire Office
Wurttembergische Feuerversicherungs AG
Yasuda Fire & Marine Insurance Co. (U.K.) Ltd.
Yorkshire Insurance Co., Ltd.

**Honorary Member**

G.W. Hogsflesh

**Affiliate Member**

The Liverpool Underwriters' Association

THE INSTITUTE OF LONDON UNDERWRITERS

# Chairmen & Deputy Chairmen

since incorporation

| | *Chairmen* | *Deputy Chairmen* |
|---|---|---|
| 1884 — 1885 | Lawrence D. Smith | Alfred W. Tozer |
| 1886 — 1887 | J. H. Lukis | Alfred W. Tozer |
| 1888 — 1894 | J. Carr Saunders | J. S. Mackintosh |
| 1895 — 1898 | J. S. Mackintosh | Akroyd Hyslop |
| 1899 | Akroyd Hyslop | T. J. Storey |
| 1900 — 1901 | T. J. Storey | Edward W. Nicholls |
| 1902 — 1903 | Edward W. Nicholls | H. Finch |
| 1904 — 1905 | H. Finch | R. B. Lemon |
| 1906 — 1908 | R. B. Lemon | S. Kennard Davis |
| 1909 | S. Kennard Davis | R. A. Ogilvie |
| 1910 — 1911 | R. A. Ogilvie | James Shaw |
| 1912 | R. B. Lemon | James Shaw |
| 1913 | Herbert T. Hines | James Shaw |
| 1914 | Herbert T. Hines | Edward F. Nicholls |
| 1915 — 1917 | Edward F. Nicholls | R. Lawton Tate |
| 1918 | Edward F. Nicholls | E. L. Jacobs |
| 1919 — 1920 | E. L. Jacobs | H. F. Kingdon |
| 1921 | H. F. Kingdon | W. E. A. Williams |
| 1922 — 1923 | W. E. A. Williams | E. L. Jacobs |
| 1924 — 1925 | Herbert T. Hines | G. G. Sharman |
| 1926 | Edward F. Nicholls | Hugh M. Merriman |
| 1927 — 1928 | Hugh M. Merriman | G. A. T. Darby |
| 1929 — 1930 | G. A. T. Darby | G. G. Sharman |
| 1931 | G. G. Sharman | E. L. Jacobs |
| 1932 | G. G. Sharman | P. H. Matthews |
| 1933 | P. H. Matthews | G. A. T. Darby |
| 1934 — 1935 | H. T. Russell Ross | R. Hall |
| 1936 — 1937 | R. Hall | A. L. Kennedy (1.1.36 to 11.10.37) A. M. Richardson (12.10.37 to 31.12.37) |
| 1938 | A. M. Richardson | G. A. T. Darby |
| 1939 | A. M. Richardson | T. R. Berridge |
| 1940 — 1941 | T. R. Berridge | H. Lloyd Owen |
| 1942 — 1943 | H. Lloyd Owen | C. E. P. Taylor |
| 1944 | C. E. P. Taylor | H. Lloyd Owen |
| 1945 | C. E. P. Taylor | Harold H. Mummery |
| 1946 — 1947 | Harold H. Mummery | E. H. N. Dowlen |
| 1948 — 1949 | E. H. N. Dowlen | A. W. Theobald |
| 1950 — 1951 | A. W. Theobald | A. Glanvill Smith |
| 1952 — 1953 | A. Glanvill Smith | L. K. Sweet |
| 1954 | L. K. Sweet | G. A. T. Darby |
| 1955 | L. K. Sweet | G. W. Hogsflesh |
| 1956 — 1957 | G. W. Hogsflesh | W. C. Shilling (1.1.56 to 30.6.57) H. Hopwood (1.7.57 to 31.12.57) |
| 1958 — 1959 | H. Hopwood | H. M. MacDiarmid |
| 1960 — 1961 | H. M. MacDiarmid | C. W. Bazell |
| 1962 | C. W. Bazell (1.1.62 to 30.6.62) | L. A. Locke |
| 1962 — 1963 | L. A. Locke (1.7.62 to 31.12.63) | P. G. L. Case |
| 1964 — 1965 | P. G. L. Case | C. E. R. Taylor |
| 1966 — 1967 | C. E. R. Taylor | G. Donald Taylor |
| 1968 — 1969 | G. Donald Taylor | S. J. Charlton |
| 1970 — 1971 | S. J. Charlton | W. J. Claydon |
| 1972 — 1973 | W. J. Claydon | E. D. Rainbow |
| 1974 — 1975 | E. D. Rainbow | A. E. Mann |
| 1976 — 1977 | A. E. Mann | B. K. Williams |
| 1978 — 1979 | B. K. Williams | H. G. Merriman |
| 1980 — 1981 | H. G. Merriman | A. S. Nunn |
| 1982 — 1983 | A. S. Nunn | D. Town |
| 1984 — | D. Town | D. D. Lowen |

THE INSTITUTE OF LONDON UNDERWRITERS

# Chief Executives

| | | |
|---|---|---|
| C. W. Emson | Secretary | 1884 — 1899 |
| C. H. Stanley | Secretary | 1900 — 1906 |
| A. S. Garfit | Secretary | 1907 — 1920 |
| G. Morrison | Secretary | 1921 — 1923 |
| E. P. Hudson | Vice Chairman & Secretary | 1923 — 1930 |
| Hugh E. Gordon | Manager & Secretary | 1931 — 1953 |
| W. H. Ridley | Manager & Secretary | 1953 — 1965 |
| A. C. Hull | Manager & Secretary | 1965 — 1979 |
| B. D. Curtis | General Manager & Secretary | 1979 — |